The Senses

THE HUMAN BODY
How It Works

Cells, Tissues, and Skin

The Circulatory System

Digestion and Nutrition

The Endocrine System

Human Development

The Immune System

The Nervous System

The Reproductive System

The Respiratory System

The Senses

The Skeletal and Muscular Systems

THE HUMAN BODY
How It Works

The Senses

Douglas B. Light

INTRODUCTION BY
Denton A. Cooley, M.D.
President and Surgeon-in-Chief
of the Texas Heart Institute
Clinical Professor of Surgery at the
University of Texas Medical School, Houston, Texas

CHELSEA HOUSE
PUBLISHERS
An imprint of Infobase Publishing

Chelsea House
An imprint of Infobase Publishing
132 West 31st Street
New York NY 10001

Library of Congress Cataloging-in-Publication Data

Light, Douglas. B.
  The Senses / Douglas B. Light.
    p. cm. — (The human body, how it works)
  Includes bibliographical references and index.
  ISBN 978-1-60413-362-2 (hardcover)
  1. Senses and sensation—Juvenile literature. I. Title. II. Series.

  QP434.L54 2009
  612.8—dc22   2009003664

Series design by Erika Arroyo, Erik Lindstrom
Cover design by Takeshi Takahashi

Printed in the United States of America

Bang EJB 10 9 8 7 6 5 4 3 2 1

This book is printed on acid-free paper.

All links and Web addresses were checked and verified to be correct at the time of publication. Because of the dynamic nature of the Web, some addresses and links may have changed since publication and may no longer be valid.

Contents

Introduction   6
Denton A. Cooley, M.D.
President and Surgeon-in-Chief
of the Texas Heart Institute
Clinical Professor of Surgery at the
University of Texas Medical School, Houston, Texas

1   **Sensory Receptors and Sensation**   10

2   **The General Senses**   22

3   **Sense of Taste**   34

4   **Sense of Smell**   45

5   **Accessory Structures of the Eye**   57

6   **Structure of the Eye**   67

7   **Sense of Sight**   79

8   **Sense of Hearing**   94

9   **Sense of Equilibrium**   109

10 **Sense of Thirst and Hunger**   116

    Appendix: Conversion Chart   131

    Glossary   132

    Bibliography   149

    Further Resources   153

    Picture Credits   159

    Index   160

    About the Author   168

Introduction

THE HUMAN BODY IS AN INCREDIBLY COMPLEX AND amazing structure. At best, it is a source of strength, beauty, and wonder. We can compare the healthy body to a well-designed machine whose parts work smoothly together. We can also compare it to a symphony orchestra in which each instrument has a different part to play. When all of the musicians play together, they produce beautiful music.

From a purely physical standpoint, our bodies are made mainly of water. We are also made of many minerals, including calcium, phosphorous, potassium, sulfur, sodium, chlorine, magnesium, and iron. In order of size, the elements of the body are organized into cells, tissues, and organs. Related organs are combined into systems, including the musculo-skeletal, cardiovascular, nervous, respiratory, gastrointestinal, endocrine, and reproductive systems.

Our cells and tissues are constantly wearing out and being replaced without our even knowing it. In fact, much of the time, we take the body for granted. When it is working properly, we tend to ignore it. Although the heart beats about 100,000 times per day and we breathe more than 10 million times per year, we do not normally think about these things. When something goes wrong, however, our bodies tell us through pain and other symptoms. In fact, pain is a very effective alarm system that lets us know the body needs attention. If the pain does not go away, we may need to see a doctor. Even without medical help, the body has an amazing ability to heal itself. If we cut ourselves, the blood-clotting system works to seal the cut right away, and the immune defense system sends out special blood cells that are programmed to heal the area.

During the past 50 years, doctors have gained the ability to repair or replace almost every part of the body. In my own field of cardiovascular surgery, we are able to open the heart and repair its valves, arteries, chambers, and connections. In many cases, these repairs can be done through a tiny "keyhole" incision that speeds up patient recovery and leaves hardly any scar. If the entire heart is diseased, we can replace it altogether, either with a donor heart or with a mechanical device. In the future, the use of mechanical hearts will probably be common in patients who would otherwise die of heart disease.

Until the mid-twentieth century, infections and contagious diseases related to viruses and bacteria were the most common causes of death. Even a simple scratch could become infected and lead to death from "blood poisoning." After penicillin and other antibiotics became available in the 1930s and 1940s, doctors were able to treat blood poisoning, tuberculosis, pneumonia, and many other bacterial diseases. Also, the introduction of modern vaccines allowed us to prevent childhood illnesses, smallpox, polio, flu, and other contagions that used to kill or cripple thousands.

Today, plagues such as the "Spanish flu" epidemic of 1918–19, which killed 20 to 40 million people worldwide, are unknown except in history books. Now that these diseases can be avoided, people are living long enough to have long-term (chronic) conditions such as cancer, heart failure, diabetes, and arthritis. Because chronic diseases tend to involve many organ systems or even the whole body, they cannot always be cured with surgery. These days, researchers are doing a lot of work at the cellular level, trying to find the underlying causes of chronic illnesses. Scientists recently finished mapping the human genome, which is a set of coded "instructions" programmed into our cells. Each cell contains 3 billion "letters" of this code. By showing how the body is made, the human genome will help researchers prevent and treat disease at its source, within the cells themselves.

The body's long-term health depends on many factors, called risk factors. Some risk factors, including our age, sex, and family history of certain diseases, are beyond our control. Other important risk factors include our lifestyle, behavior, and environment. Our modern lifestyle offers many advantages but is not always good for our bodies. In western Europe and the United States, we tend to be stressed, overweight, and out of shape. Many of us have unhealthy habits such as smoking cigarettes, abusing alcohol, or using drugs. Our air, water, and food often contain hazardous chemicals and industrial waste products. Fortunately, we can do something about most of these risk factors. At any age, the most important things we can do for our bodies are to eat right, exercise regularly, get enough sleep, and refuse to smoke, overuse alcohol, or use addictive drugs. We can also help clean up our environment. These simple steps will lower our chances of getting cancer, heart disease, or other serious disorders.

These days, thanks to the Internet and other forms of media coverage, people are more aware of health-related matters. The average person knows more about the human body than ever before. Patients want to understand their medical conditions and treatment options. They want to play a more active role, along with their doctors, in making medical decisions and in taking care of their own health.

I encourage you to learn as much as you can about your body and to treat your body well. These things may not seem too important to you now, while you are young, but the habits and behaviors that you practice today will affect your physical well-being for the rest of your life. The present book series, THE HUMAN BODY: HOW IT WORKS, is an excellent introduction to human biology and anatomy. I hope that it will awaken within you a lifelong interest in these subjects.

Denton A. Cooley, M.D.
President and Surgeon-in-Chief
of the Texas Heart Institute
Clinical Professor of Surgery at the
University of Texas Medical School, Houston, Texas

1

Sensory Receptors and Sensation

THE HUMAN BRAIN IS TRULY AN AMAZING ORGAN. ALTHOUGH it weighs only about 1.4 kilograms (3 pounds), this highly organized collection of cells lets us communicate with others, perform mental tasks, remember homework assignments, understand concepts, be aware of our surroundings, and move our body parts. However, the brain would be useless without its connections to the rest of the body and to the outside world. In fact, as strange as it sounds, we do not experience our environment and the events taking place within our bodies directly or in their entirety. Instead, we experience them by way of specialized sense organs that send information to the brain. In other words, just about everything we know about the world comes to us through our senses, and everything we do depends on receiving and correctly interpreting information from our external and internal environments.

SENSATION AND PERCEPTION

Both sensation and perception are functions of the brain—specifically, a part of the brain called the **cerebral cortex**, or cerebrum (Figure 1.1). Nerve impulses from sensory receptors are transmitted to particular parts of the brain. The brain interprets them as **sensations,** an awareness and localization of

10

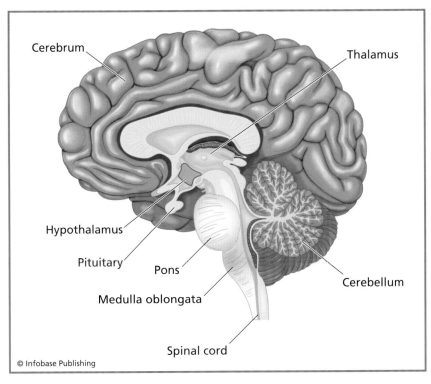

Cerebrum

Thalamus

Hypothalamus

Pituitary

Pons

Medulla oblongata

Cerebellum

Spinal cord

© Infobase Publishing

Figure 1.1 The outermost layer of the brain is the cerebral cortex (cerebrum), a layer of gray matter about 2 to 4 millimeters (0.08 to 0.16 inches) thick. It is in the cerebrum that the brain identifies and interprets sensations.

a stimulus. A **stimulus** is a change in the internal or external environment that leads to a response. A **perception** involves giving meaning to a sensation based on what we have experienced and learned. For instance, stepping on a tack will cause a sensation of pain, whereas an awareness of being injured would be considered a perception. Perception is important in determining how we will respond to a particular stimulus.

THE ROLE OF SENSORY RECEPTORS

Sensations, and the perceptions they evoke, begin with **sensory reception**, the detection of a stimulus (or, more accurately, the energy of a stimulus) by sensory receptors. **Sensory receptors** are anatomical structures made up of special cells that respond to specific changes in their environment (stimuli). In so doing, they provide the central nervous system (brain and spinal cord) with information about conditions both inside and outside the body. In this way, sensory receptors are the physical links between your central nervous system and the environment (Figure 1.2).

TRANSDUCTION AND RECEPTOR POTENTIALS

Sensory receptors work by first detecting a stimulus and then translating that energy into electrical signals, which are conducted by nerve cells, or **neurons**, to the central nervous

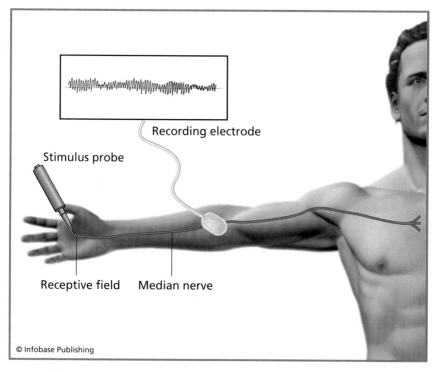

© Infobase Publishing

Figure 1.2 Scientists have different ways of testing human sensory receptors. A researcher may probe a person's hand with an electrical signal to stimulate it and record how often parts of the brain send and receive signals about the sensation. The median nerve of the arm transmits the impulses from the sensory receptors of the hand to the brain.

system. Turning a stimulus into an electrical signal is called **transduction** (a transducer is a device that changes one form of energy into another). Specialized sensory receptors are needed to detect stimuli because the brain has no such ability. That is, the brain is designed to receive electrical signals from the nervous system; beyond that, it is essentially "blind" to all other forms of stimuli. This explains why neurosurgeons may perform procedures on the brain of an awake patient. Only a local anesthetic is needed for the scalp because the brain cannot directly sense touch or pain.

The initial response of a sensory receptor to a stimulus is to change its cell membrane permeability to ions—how many and what kinds of ions it lets through. In other words, in response to an appropriate stimulus, transport pathways for specific ions open and/or close, depending on the type of stimulus and receptor (Figure 1.3). This, in turn, influences the movement of a charge across the cell membrane, resulting in a graded change in the membrane potential (voltage), which is called a **receptor potential**. The magnitude of a receptor potential is directly related to how strong the stimulus is. If a receptor potential is large enough, it may result in a conscious sensation by the brain (that is, a conscious awareness of the stimulus). However, much of the sensory information that goes to the central nervous system is filtered out by specific parts of the brain; as a result, no sensation is perceived for many stimuli. This is important because the brain would otherwise be overloaded with too many signals to sort through. For instance, we are usually not aware of our muscle tension or blood pH levels (pH meaning a measurement of the acidity or alkalinity of a solution). We also have the ability to listen to a friend in a noisy restaurant, while simultaneously "tuning out" the myriad of other conversations and sounds around us.

SENSORY MODALITY AND RECEPTOR SPECIFICITY

We are able to distinguish a variety of sensory stimuli because each kind of stimulus activates different types of

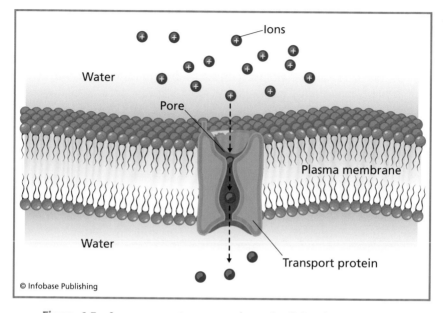

Figure 1.3 Sensory receptors respond to stimuli by changing the permeability of their cell membranes to let in or keep out specific ions. They do this with the help of transport proteins, which create pores that allow the passage of certain ions through the membrane.

receptor cells. The term **modality** refers to the type of sensation a stimulus produces. Each category of sensation, such as touch, taste, or sound, is a sensory modality. The features that characterize stimuli within a certain modality are called "qualities." For instance, light can be red or blue, taste can be sweet or sour, and sounds can be high or low in pitch.

Each receptor has its own special sensitivity to stimuli. For example, a receptor for light does not react to sound waves, and a taste receptor that responds to dissolved chemicals does not respond to light. This concept of receptors responding only to a particular stimulus is called **receptor specificity**. Interestingly, and amazingly, many receptors can detect the smallest physical unit of stimulus possible. For example, some receptor cells of the nose can respond to a single molecule of odor! The receptor cells of the inner ear can sense motion of only a few angstroms (about the size of a single water molecule), and many photoreceptor cells can detect a single quantum (photon) of light.

Receptors can be categorized in different ways based on:

(1) the type of sensation (modality) to which they respond,
(2) the location of the stimulus to which they respond, and
(3) their structural complexity.

CLASSIFICATION OF RECEPTORS BY MODALITY

Receptors that respond to chemicals in solution are called **chemoreceptors**. Some chemoreceptors are general receptors that detect information about the total number of dissolved substances in a solution. For instance, **osmoreceptors** in your brain are chemoreceptors that sense changes in the total

DID YOU KNOW?

Sensory organs are the only channels of communication between the brain and the outside world. Simply put, the brain is not designed to sense on its own. For instance, an exposed brain would neither sense light shining on it nor feel something touching it. In fact, patients are often kept awake during brain surgery, which can help a surgeon isolate specific regions of the brain. The ancient Greek philosopher Aristotle recognized this characteristic of the brain over 2,000 years ago when he said, "Nothing is in the mind that does not pass through the senses." This concept can be seen clearly when volunteers are blindfolded and placed in the warm water of a sensory deprivation tank. They soon experience visual, auditory, and tactile (touch) hallucinations, as well as incoherent thought patterns. From these experiments and others, it is apparent that we need constant input from our senses to carry out functions that give us personality and intellect.

solute (dissolved substances) concentration of the blood and make you thirsty when this concentration increases. In contrast, other types of chemoreceptors respond to individual kinds of molecules. In this case, the stimulus molecule binds to a specific site on the membrane of the receptor cell, which leads to changes in membrane permeability and alters the membrane potential. The chemoreceptors involved with taste and smell are of this type.

Receptors that respond to light are called **photoreceptors**. The eye contains two kinds of photoreceptors: rods (for vision in dim light) and cones (for color vision). **Thermoreceptors** are sensitive to temperature changes and react to either heat or cold. The body, in turn, uses this information to regulate both its surface and core (internal) temperature. Receptors that are stimulated by touch, pressure, stretch, tension, or vibration are called **mechanoreceptors**. These include receptors in the organs for hearing and balance (located in the inner ear) and many receptors in the skin, viscera (internal organs), and joints. Muscle spindle fibers are specialized mechanoreceptors, called stretch receptors, that monitor the length of skeletal muscles.

Receptors that respond to potentially damaging stimuli and cause pain are called **nociceptors**. Stimuli that influence nociceptors include trauma from blows or cuts, ischemia (poor blood flow), and too much stimulation by heat, radiation, and chemicals. Although, for some people, chronic pain can be debilitating, the sensation of pain is necessary for survival because the stimulus that causes pain often translates into a defensive reaction or withdrawal from danger. Imagine how difficult it would be for you to survive if you lacked the ability to sense pain. Without a sense of pain, you wouldn't know when you should pull your hand away from a hot stove or a sharp knife.

CLASSIFICATION OF RECEPTORS BY LOCATION

Receptors may also be classified according to the location of the stimulus to which they respond. Receptors that detect stimuli that come from inside the body, such as those from the internal organs and blood vessels, are called **interoceptors**. They monitor a variety of stimuli, including chemical changes in body fluids, tissue stretch, and body temperature. Although we are usually unaware of the workings of interoceptors, they sometimes can produce feelings of visceral pain, nausea, stretch, pressure, hunger, or thirst. **Exteroceptors**, on the other hand, respond to stimuli coming from outside the body. They include receptors for touch, pressure, pain, temperature, vision, hearing, taste, and smell. **Proprioceptors** are located in skeletal muscles, tendons, and joints, and in the ligaments and connective tissue that cover the bones and muscles. They are important for sensing the position and movements of the body and its parts.

CLASSIFICATION OF RECEPTORS BY STRUCTURAL COMPLEXITY

Another way to classify receptors is by the complexity of their structure. The majority of receptors are considered **simple receptors**, which means that they are made up of the modified nerve endings, or **dendrites.** Simple receptors involve **sensory neurons,** which send signals from receptors to the brain and spinal cord. Simple receptors are found throughout the body and monitor most types of **general senses**, which include tactile sensation (touch, pressure, stretch, and vibration), temperature (heat and cold), and pain. In contrast, **complex receptors** are those we think of as the classical **sense organs**: localized collections of cells associated with the **special senses** (hearing, balance, smell, vision, and taste).

SENSORY RECEPTOR TRANSMISSION

Sensory receptors transmit four kinds of information: modality, location, intensity, and duration. As stated previously, modality is the type of sensation produced by a stimulus, such as vision, hearing, or taste. However, the actual nerve impulses that reach the brain from virtually all kinds of receptors are identical in nature. How, then, does the brain distinguish between different modalities if the input it receives is the same from all receptors? It does this by having nerve impulses arrive via different nerve fibers, which, in turn, stimulate different centers in the brain. This arrangement is referred to as a **labeled line code**. In essence, the brain has a number of "lines" (nerve fibers) that deliver information, which might loosely be compared to phone lines. Just as each phone line handles a different

DID YOU KNOW?

You can reduce the perception of pain if you take certain drugs. Two common over-the-counter **analgesics** (painkillers) are aspirin and ibuprofen. They decrease pain by inhibiting the body's production of chemicals called **prostaglandins**, which cause pain by making receptors more sensitive. Thus, aspirin and ibuprofen essentially lower the number of signals that go to the brain from pain receptors. In contrast, the much stronger drug morphine acts directly on receptors in the brain so that incoming signals are not sensed and perceived.

General anesthesia, commonly used during certain medical and surgical procedures, refers to the induction of a state of unconsciousness with the absence of pain sensation over the entire body through the administration of anesthetic drugs. The purpose of general anesthesia is not just analgesia (pain relief) but also amnesia (blocking of memory of the medical procedure), unconsciousness, and inhibition of normal body reflexes (to make the surgery easier to perform). It is not known exactly how general anesthetics work, but it is thought that they alter the flow of sodium ions across cell membranes into nerve cells, thereby inhibiting nerve impulses. In this way, the brain becomes unconscious, does not store memories, does not register pain impulses from other areas of the body, and does not control involuntary reflexes. It should be noted that anesthesia is not the same as sleep.

conversation, each nerve fiber represents a specific modality. In other words, even though all the nerve impulses arriving in the brain are similar in nature (all are electrical signals), the impulses that arrive on one nerve fiber have a different meaning for the brain than impulses arriving on another. For instance, any nerve impulses that go to the brain from the optic nerve from the eye are interpreted as light. This helps explain why a blow to the eye, which can stimulate the optic nerve, may initially be perceived as a flash of light rather than pain. Imagine what would happen to perception if the nerve fibers leaving receptors were somehow mixed up before they arrived at the brain.

The location of a stimulus is encoded by the specific nerve fibers that are firing. That is, the brain has the ability to tell where the stimulus is coming from based on information carried by nerve fibers. This ability is termed **sensory projection**. Sometimes the brain can be fooled, however. One example is **phantom pain**—the perception of a feeling of pain in a limb after it has been surgically amputated. Phantom pain demonstrates that sensory projection is a process that occurs in the brain—not at the level of the receptor. The brain also can determine how intense a stimulus is based on the number and kinds of nerve fibers that are firing and also on the amount of time between stimuli.

RECEPTOR ADAPTATION

Many types of receptors have the ability to change their frequency of firing over time in response to a constant stimulus. This process, called **adaptation**, refers to a decrease in responsiveness of receptors to continued stimulation. **Phasic receptors** generate a burst of activity when they are first stimulated and then quickly stop transmitting impulses even if the stimulus continues (in other words, they adapt quickly). Tactile receptors in the skin and hair receptors are two examples of rapidly adapting phasic receptors. If these receptors were not phasic, we would sense a continual barrage of stimuli. For instance, without sensory adaptation, you would feel every bit of clothing on your body all day long.

In contrast to phasic receptors, **tonic receptors** adapt slowly and therefore generate nerve impulses continually. Proprioceptors—receptors located in skeletal muscles, tendons, and joints—are among the most slowly adapting tonic receptors. This is significant because the brain must always be aware of body position, muscle tension, and joint motions.

CONNECTIONS

A sensation is the awareness and localization of a stimulus (a change in the internal or external environment that evokes a response). Once the brain is aware of sensations, it interprets them, helping us perceive what the stimulus is. Sensations and the perceptions they evoke begin with sensory reception, the detection of a stimulus by sensory cells and its transduction into an electrical signal. We are able to tell different types of sensory stimuli apart because they selectively activate different specialized types of receptor cells.

Receptors that respond to chemicals in solution are called chemoreceptors, whereas those that respond to light energy are known as photoreceptors. Thermoreceptors are sensitive to temperature changes, and those that are stimulated by physical deformation are called mechanoreceptors. Nociceptors respond to potentially damaging stimuli and cause pain.

Receptors that detect stimuli arising from within the body are called interoceptors. They monitor a variety of stimuli, including chemical changes in body fluids, tissue stretch, and body temperature. In contrast, exteroceptors respond to stimuli coming from outside the body, and proprioceptors are located in skeletal muscles, tendons, and joints.

Sensory receptors transmit four kinds of information: modality, location, intensity, and duration. This is accomplished, in part, by having nerve impulses arrive in the brain via different nerve fibers, thereby stimulating different brain centers. This arrangement is termed a labeled line code.

Receptors can change how often they fire over time in response to a constant stimulus. This process is called adaptation, and it refers to a decrease in the responsiveness of receptors during continued stimulation. Phasic receptors generate a burst of activity when first stimulated and then quickly stop sending impulses even if the stimulus continues. In contrast, tonic receptors adapt slowly and therefore generate nerve impulses continually.

2

The General Senses

THE RECEPTORS FOR THE GENERAL SENSES ARE SCATTERED throughout the body and are relatively simple in structure. They consist of one or a few sensory nerve fibers and usually a sparse amount of connective tissue that enhances their sensitivity or how specific their responses are. The general sensory receptors are involved in tactile sensation (touch, pressure, stretch, and vibration), temperature monitoring (heat and cold), and pain, as well as muscle tension and joint position. They can be classified according to whether they have unencapsulated or capsulated nerve endings.

UNENCAPSULATED NERVE ENDINGS

Unencapsulated nerve endings are nerve endings that are not wrapped in connective tissue. They are found nearly everywhere in the body, but are especially abundant in epithelial tissues (such as skin) and tissues that hold body parts together (such as tendons and ligaments). Most of these sensory nerves are fibers that are small in diameter and have no special association with accessory cells or tissues, although their ends usually have small, knoblike swellings. Among this type of sensory nerves are warmth receptors, which respond to rising temperatures; cold receptors, which respond to falling temperatures; and nociceptors, which sense pain.

Some unencapsulated nerve endings are associated with enlarged, disk-shaped epidermal (skin) cells called Merkel cells and form **Merkel's disks**, which lie in the deep layers of the epidermis, the outermost layer of the skin (Figure 2.1). These structures are tonic receptors, which adapt slowly, for light touch and are thought to help us sense different textures, edges, and shapes.

Other free nerve endings, called **root hair plexuses**, monitor the movement of hairs by wrapping around hair follicles. They respond to any light touch that bends a hair. For instance, when a mosquito lands on your skin or an ant crawls on the back of your neck they bend hairs, and this is detected by root hair plexuses. Because this type of receptor adapts quickly, we

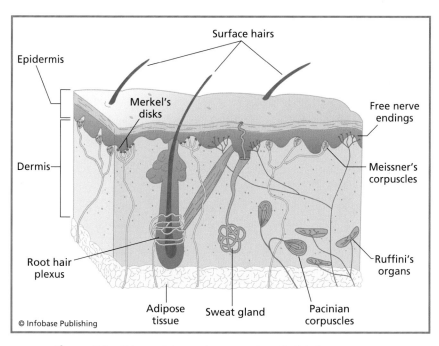

Figure 2.1 Skin contains various receptors that help us sense our environment. Merkel's disks, Meissner's corpuscles, and Ruffini's organs (or corpuscles), for example, sense light touches and pressure, while Pacinian corpuscles sense vibration.

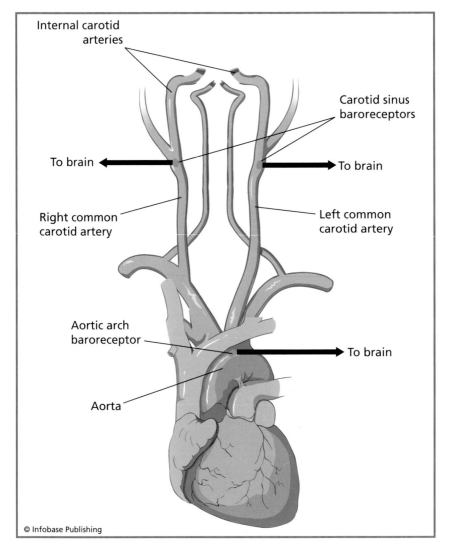

Internal carotid arteries

Carotid sinus baroreceptors

To brain

To brain

Right common carotid artery

Left common carotid artery

Aortic arch baroreceptor

To brain

Aorta

© Infobase Publishing

Figure 2.2 Baroreceptors are found in the carotid sinuses and aortic arch. When the blood pressure in the arteries rises and stretches these receptors, they send a rapid stream of signals to the central nervous system. This may cause the blood vessels to dilate, lowering blood pressure.

are not constantly aware of our clothing, even though it continually bends our body hairs.

Some unencapsulated nerve endings branch within the "elastic" walls of organs, which can expand. Elastic walls are found in blood vessels and organs of the digestive, urinary, and respiratory tracts. The unencapsulated nerve endings, which are called **baroreceptors,** monitor changes in pressure (Figure 2.2). These receptors respond immediately to changes in pressure, but they also adapt rapidly. Baroreceptors are especially important for regulating blood pressure. They are found in the walls of major blood vessels, such as the carotid artery (which delivers oxygen-rich blood to the brain) and the aorta (the major artery carrying blood from the heart to the body tissues). Baroreceptors in the digestive system provide information on the volume of organs and also trigger reflexes that move materials through the digestive tract. Similarly, stretch receptors in the wall of the urinary bladder give us information about the volume of the bladder and also are involved with triggering urination. Baroreceptors in the lungs monitor the degree of lung expansion and help prevent the lungs from stretching too much. They also help regulate the smooth rhythm of breathing.

As mentioned previously, unencapsulated nerve endings called chemoreceptors detect small changes in the concentration of specific chemicals. These receptors do not send information to the primary sensory cortex of the brain, so we are not consciously aware of the sensations they provide. Instead, their signals go to parts of the brain that deal with **autonomic** (unconscious) control over breathing and cardiovascular functions. Some important chemoreceptors are located in the aorta and in the carotid bodies, structures near the origin of the carotid arteries. These particular chemoreceptors monitor levels of carbon dioxide and hydrogen ions (acid) in the blood, which helps the brain control how fast and how deeply we breathe. There also are chemoreceptors in the brain that respond to levels of acid in the cerebrospinal fluid, the liquid that fills the space in and around the brain and spinal cord.

ENCAPSULATED NERVE ENDINGS

All **encapsulated nerve endings** consist of one or more endings of sensory nerves that are wrapped in special connective tissue, which enhances the sensitivity and specificity of the

receptor. Virtually all of these receptors are mechanoreceptors for touch, pressure, and stretch. However, they vary in
shape, size, and distribution in the body.

Meissner's corpuscles are phasic receptors for light touch
and texture (see Figure 2.1). They are found just beneath the
epidermis in the **dermal papillae** and are especially numerous in sensitive and hairless skin areas, such as the fingertips,
palms of the hands, soles of the feet, eyelids, lips, nipples, and
genitals. They are oval in shape and fairly large, about 100
micrometers (μm; 0.004 inches) long and 50 μm (0.002 in.)
wide. The dendrites of these cells are highly coiled and are surrounded by modified **Schwann cells**, a type of cell that forms
insulation around nerve fibers. A fibrous capsule wraps around
the entire complex, which anchors it within the dermis.

Meissner's corpuscles are sensitive to fine touch and pressure, as well as to low-frequency vibration. They enable us
to tell the difference between a smooth texture, such as silk,
and a rough surface, like sandpaper. Tactile receptors play
essentially the same role in light touch reception in hairless
skin that the root hair plexuses play in hairy skin. Meissner's
corpuscles adapt quickly to stimulation, usually within just one
second after contact. **Krause end bulbs** are similar to Meissner's
corpuscles in their sensitivity to touch, but they are found in
mucous membranes rather than in the skin.

Pacinian corpuscles are phasic receptors for deep pressure,
stretch, tickle, and vibration (see Figure 2.1). They are scattered
in the dermis of the skin and in the tissue beneath it, and
are especially numerous in the hands, feet, breasts, and
genitals. Pacinian corpuscles consist of a single nerve ending
surrounded by up to 60 concentric layers of connective tissue.
In cross-section, they look something like a sliced onion. They
are the largest of the corpuscular receptors, and may reach 3 to
4 millimeters (mm) (0.16 in.) in length and 1 mm (0.04 in.)
in diameter (large enough to be seen with the naked eye). The
concentric layers shield the dendrite from virtually all sources
of stimulation other than direct pressure. Although these

receptors are stimulated by deep pressure, they respond only when a stimulus is first applied, and then they adapt quickly. Thus, Pacinian corpuscles are best suited to sense vibrations.

DID YOU KNOW?

Unencapsulated nerve endings are responsible, at least in part, for itch and tickle sensations, which are transmitted to the central nervous system by small-diameter, unmyelinated nerve fibers. Itch receptors consist of unencapsulated nerve endings located in the dermis, the inner layer of the skin. There are many of them inside the surfaces of the eyelids and the mucous membranes of the nose. However, there are no itch sensations in other mucous membranes or in deep tissues and viscera (internal organs). Itch receptors can be directly stimulated by certain chemicals, such as histamine and other agents released by white blood cells during inflammation. This explains why the administration of an antihistamine or cortisone, agents that stop white blood cells from releasing some chemicals, helps make inflamed areas less itchy.

Tickle sensations are produced by a light touch that moves across the skin and are probably caused by the stimulation of itch receptors. Psychological factors (such as the person's mood) are also involved in the perception of tickle sensations. Different people have very different levels of tickle sensitivity. This is why some people are so much more "ticklish" than others.

How does scratching relieve an itch or tickle? In part, the back and forth movement may simply remove an irritant, thereby relieving an itch. In addition, a scratch may be sufficiently strong to suppress itch signals in the spinal cord by a process called lateral inhibition (that is, when skin is touched, several sensory neurons are stimulated, which may suppress the stimulation of neighboring nerve cells so that only the most stimulated neurons fire). Interestingly, a recent study indicates that areas of the brain associated with unpleasant or aversive emotions and memories become significantly less active during scratching (this might also explain the compulsion to continue scratching).

Ruffini's corpuscles are tonic receptors for heavy touch, pressure, stretching of the skin, and joint movements (see Figure 2.1). They lie beneath the skin and inside ligaments, tendons, and joints, and respond to deep and continuous pressure. They look like long, flattened capsules containing a few nerve fibers intertwined with collagen fibers. Any tension or distortion of the dermis tugs and twists the capsular fibers, stretching or squeezing the attached dendrites, which leads to a change in their membrane potential. Ruffini's corpuscles are tonic receptors, showing little adaptation.

Muscle spindles are proprioceptors (from *prioprius,* meaning "one's own") found throughout skeletal muscles. Each muscle spindle is a bundle of 3 to 10 intrafusal fibers, which are modified skeletal muscle fibers, enclosed within a connective tissue capsule. These intrafusal fibers are about one-fourth the diameter of normal muscle fibers. The central region of an intrafusal fiber lacks the ability to contract. Instead, these structures act as receptive surfaces, since they are wrapped

DID YOU KNOW?

As mentioned earlier, pain plays an important role in survival because it makes us aware of potential injuries or actual injuries. Without pain, we would ignore simple cuts and splinters, which could lead to more serious infections. A good example of the protective function of pain is seen in people with leprosy (Hansen's disease). This condition, characterized by severe deformity of the hands, feet, and face, is caused by a bacterium (*Mycobacterium leprae*) that infects nerves, resulting in a loss of pain and other sensations in the affected areas. As a result, victims often fail to notice minor injuries, such as scrapes, cuts, splinters, and burns. Neglecting these wounds leads to serious infections that damage deep tissue, including bone. In fact, it is common for people with leprosy to have some of their fingers and toes amputated because minor injuries have progressed to the point of developing necrosis (tissue death).

with sensory nerves that lead to the central nervous system. In this way, intrafusal fibers can tell when a muscle stretches; it can then initiate a reflex that resists further stretch.

For instance, in a knee-jerk reflex, a doctor's mallet striking the patellar tendon stretches the quadriceps muscle, stimulating intrafusal fibers in the muscle spindles, which then send impulses to the spinal cord. This stimulates the spinal cord to initiate impulses that are sent back to the leg, causing contraction of the stretched muscle and thereby reversing the initial stretch. Interestingly, this particular reflex involves only two neurons (nerve cells), one going to the spinal cord (a sensory neuron) and one returning to the quadriceps (a motor neuron).

Golgi tendon organs are proprioceptors found in tendons, close to the point where a tendon fuses with a skeletal muscle. They consist of small bundles of collagen fibers enclosed in a layered capsule, with dendrites coiling between and around the fibers (structurally, they look like Ruffini's corpuscles). Golgi tendon organs help regulate the length of skeletal muscles by monitoring the tension produced when muscles contract; they are stimulated when a muscle contracts and stretches a tendon. This, in turn, prevents the tearing or breaking of tendons.

DID YOU KNOW?

We all have the same physical threshold for pain. That is, different people's receptors all respond to painful stimuli at the same intensity. For example, we sense heat as painful at 44° to 46°C (111° to 115°F), the range at which it begins to damage tissue. However, our reactions to pain, or pain tolerance, vary widely and are influenced by cultural, emotional, and psychological factors. This is why someone involved in a disaster may feel no pain while struggling to save him- or herself or others, even if he or she actually has severe injuries. In some cultures, like India, for example, people sometimes walk over hot coals to demonstrate their mastery over pain. Interestingly, pain tolerance seems to increase with age.

PAIN RECEPTION

Pain is not just an annoying sensation; it makes us aware of potentially hazardous situations so we can avoid injury. It also makes us aware of tissue injuries so that we can try to protect the injured region. Pain is not simply due to an overstimulation of other receptors. Instead, it has its own set of receptors—**nociceptors**—that have large receptive fields (which may make it difficult to determine the exact source of a painful sensation). Nociceptors are especially common in the skin and mucous membranes, joint capsules, the outer lining of bones, and around the walls of blood vessels. There also are some nociceptors located in deep tissues and in most of the visceral organs. However, there are no nociceptors in the brain.

There are two types of nociceptors. Some belong to nerves that are surrounded by a **myelin sheath**, an insulating layer made up of Schwann cells. This sheath allows these nerves to conduct signals at rapid speeds, up to 80 meters per second (260 ft/s). Consequently, they produce the sensation known as **fast pain**. We feel this as sharp, localized, stabbing pain perceived at the time of injury. In contrast, nociceptors that are part of nerves without a myelin sheath send their signals at much slower speeds, from 0.5 to 2.0 m/s (1.6 to 6.6 ft/s). These receptors are responsible for **slow pain**—a longer-lasting, dull, diffuse feeling of pain following an injury.

Pain is classified by its point of origin. **Somatic pain** arises from the skin, muscles, or joints. It can be either superficial or deep. Superficial somatic pain is a sharp, stabbing, pricking pain that often causes us to cry out. It is transmitted to the brain by myelinated fibers—fibers encased in a myelin sheath—and is usually brief and localized to the skin epidermis and mucous membranes. In contrast, deep somatic pain is less localized, longer lasting, and more likely to be experienced as burning, itching, or aching. It results from stimulation of pain receptors in the deep skin layers, muscles, or joints, and indicates that tissue destruction is occurring. Deep somatic pain signals are sent to the brain by unmyelinated fibers.

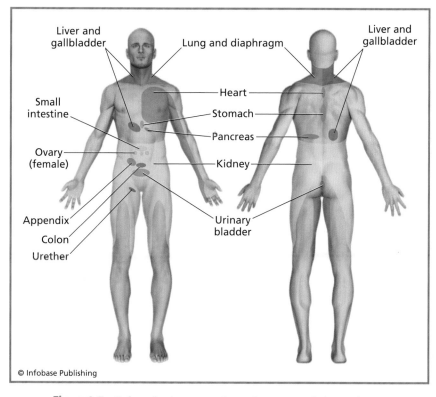

Liver and gallbladder

Lung and diaphragm

Liver and gallbladder

Small intestine

Heart

Stomach

Pancreas

Ovary (female)

Kidney

Appendix

Colon

Urether

Urinary bladder

© Infobase Publishing

Figure 2.3 Referred pain occurs when pain receptors in internal organs send signals to the brain along the same pathways that other body parts, such as skin and muscles, use. Because the body and skin feel pain much more often than organs, the brain may perceive pain from internal organs as coming from skin or muscle rather than from the actual organ. This diagram pinpoints locations at which the brain perceives there is pain when a specific organ is actually the source of pain.

Visceral pain results from noxious (harmful) stimulation of receptors in the organs of the thorax (chest) and abdominal cavity. Like deep somatic pain, it usually consists of a dull ache or a burning feeling and often includes nausea. Although it may be intense, it is poorly localized because the viscera themselves have relatively few nociceptors. Visceral pain arises from extreme stretching of tissues, chemical irritants, muscle spasms, or **ischemia** (deficient blood flow).

Because visceral pain inputs to the central nervous system follow the same pathways as somatic pain, the brain may perceive visceral pain as somatic in origin. This phenomenon is known as **referred pain** (Figure 2.3). For example, people who suffer heart attacks often feel pain radiating along the left shoulder and left arm even though it is really coming from the heart. Because the skin has more pain receptors than the heart and also experiences injuries far more often, the brain assumes that signals arriving on that labeled line are coming from the skin, even when the heart is the actual source. That is why it is important for doctors to know about referred pain and which internal organs link to other body parts so that they can better diagnose an organ dysfunction.

CONNECTIONS

Unencapsulated nerve endings are not wrapped in connective tissue and are found nearly everywhere in the body. Merkel's disks, which lie in the deeper layers of the skin epidermis, are tonic receptors for light touch. Other unencapsulated nerve endings, called root hair plexuses, monitor the movement of hairs by wrapping around hair follicles.

Some free nerve endings, called baroreceptors, are especially important for monitoring blood pressure, providing information on the volume of organs, moving materials through the digestive tract, causing urination, and regulating the expansion of the lungs. Chemoreceptors detect small changes in the concentration of specific chemicals.

Encapsulated nerve endings consist of one or more fiber terminals of sensory nerves enclosed in a connective tissue capsule, which enhances the sensitivity and specificity of the receptor. Virtually all of these receptors are mechanoreceptors for touch, pressure, and stretch. Meissner's corpuscles, phasic receptors for light touch and texture, are found just beneath the skin epidermis in the dermal papillae. These tactile receptors are sensitive to fine touch and pressure, as well as to low-frequency vibrations. Krause end bulbs are similar to Meissner's corpuscles in terms of their sensitivity to touch, but they are found in mucous membranes. Pacinian corpuscles are phasic receptors for deep pressure, stretch, tickle, and vibration. They are scattered in the dermis of the skin and in the tissue under it. These receptors are best at monitoring vibration. Ruffini's corpuscles are tonic receptors for heavy touch, pressure, stretching of the skin, and joint movements. They lie deep within the skin and in subcutaneous (under the skin) tissue, ligaments, tendons, and joint capsules, and respond to deep and continuous pressure. Ruffini's corpuscles show little adaptation.

Muscle spindles are proprioceptors found throughout skeletal muscles. They contain intrafusal fibers enclosed within a connective tissue capsule and act as receptive surfaces by being wrapped with sensory nerves that lead to the central nervous system. In this way, intrafusal fibers detect muscle stretch and cause a reflex that resists further stretch. Golgi tendon organs are proprioceptors located in tendons. They help regulate the length of skeletal muscles by monitoring the tension produced when muscles contract.

Nociceptors are unencapsulated nerve endings with large receptive fields and are especially common in the skin and mucous membranes, joint capsules, the outer lining of bones, and around the walls of blood vessels. Some nociceptors belong to nerves that are surrounded by a myelin sheath, an insulating layer made of Schwann cells. This sheath allows the nerves to conduct signals at rapid speeds and produce the sensation known as fast pain. In contrast, nociceptors that are part of nerves without a myelin sheath conduct at much slower speeds and are responsible for slow pain—a longer-lasting, dull, diffuse feeling of pain following an injury.

Pain is also classified by its point of origin. Somatic pain arises from the skin, muscles, or joints. Visceral pain results from noxious stimulation of receptors in the organs of the thorax and abdominal cavity. Because sensations of visceral pain follow the same pathways as somatic pain, projection by the brain may cause visceral pain to be perceived as somatic in origin, a phenomenon known as referred pain.

3

Sense of Taste

Gustation, THE SENSE OF TASTE, IS CONDUCTED BY chemoreceptors that respond to chemicals dissolved in the watery solution in our mouths. Gustation is important because it provides information about the quality of the food and liquid we consume. Most importantly, it helps us determine whether the items we place in our mouths should be swallowed or rejected. In fact, the word *taste* comes from the Latin word *taxare*, which means "to feel," "touch," or "judge," suggesting *taste* originally meant "to test by touching."

LOCATION OF TASTE RECEPTORS

The receptor organs for gustation, the **taste buds**, are structures composed of specialized epithelial cells. Taste buds are found in the mouth, with most of them located on the superior (upper) surface of the tongue. However, a few taste buds are also found in the pharynx (throat), soft palate, and epiglottis. As we age, these nonlingual (nontongue) taste buds decrease in number and importance. (Believe it or not, flies can actually taste with the terminal portion of their legs, as well as with the tip of the proboscis, because they have taste cells located in those regions.)

The tongue has epithelial folds and bumps called **lingual papillae**, peglike projections that give the tongue a slightly rough feel (Figure 3.1). There are four types of lingual papillae on the human tongue; however, only three of these have taste buds. **Foliate papillae** are arranged as closely packed folds along the back edges of the tongue. They are well developed in children but are much less prominent and numerous in adults. In fact, many of these taste buds degenerate by the time a person is two or three years old. **Fungiform papillae** are mushroom-shaped structures. They are the only papillae scattered over the entire surface of the tongue, and they are most numerous at the tip and sides of the tongue. These papillae usually contain two to five taste buds located on their outer surface. **Circumvallate papillae** are the largest papillae in size, and each contains about

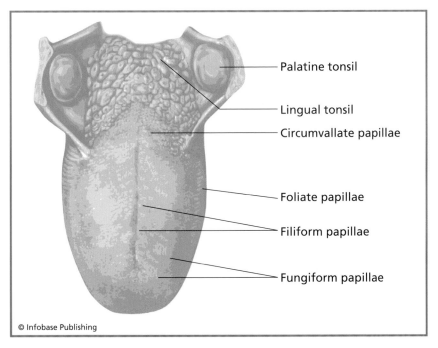

Palatine tonsil

Lingual tonsil

Circumvallate papillae

Foliate papillae

Filiform papillae

Fungiform papillae

© Infobase Publishing

Figure 3.1   The surface of the tongue is covered with several kinds of papillae, which look like tiny pegs. Some kinds of papillae contain taste buds, the receptors for the sense of gustation.

250 taste buds. Humans typically have 7 to 12 circumvallate papillae, arranged in the shape of an upside down "V" at the back of the tongue. **Filiform papillae** look like tiny bumps that cover the surface of the tongue. Although they are the most numerous papillae, they play no sensory role because they have no taste buds. They are especially prominent (and rough) in cats. Many mammals use them to groom their fur.

Embedded in the connective tissue below the circumvallate and foliate papillae are **serous glands**. These glands have ducts that open into the depressions between adjacent papillae and also between papillae and the wall of the tongue. Their secretions wash away particles of food and microorganisms.

TASTE BUDS

Regardless of location, all taste buds have a similar structure and thus look alike (Figure 3.2). Each one consists of 40 to 100 epithelial cells and is about 50 μm (0.002 in.) in diameter. Taste buds are composed of three major cell types: sensory cells, basal cells, and supporting cells.

One kind of sensory cell is the **gustatory cell**—a slender, banana-shaped cell that bears microscopic hairs (microvilli). These microvilli are called **taste hairs** and are covered with taste receptors. During chewing, water-soluble substances from food dissolve in saliva and enter a **taste pore** of a taste bud. There, they contact the taste receptors of the microvilli. Interestingly, the sensory cells (the taste receptors in this case) are not neurons; they are epithelial cells that synapse (connect) with nerve fibers at their base. These nerve fibers then send a signal to the brain that lets it know that a particular substance is present.

Despite being located within a protective pore, gustatory cells are still subject to a lot of damage from friction and from hot foods. Consequently, a typical gustatory cell lives only about 7 to 10 days. Gustatory cells are continually replaced by nearby **basal cells**, which divide and then turn into new supporting cells and gustatory cells. During the changeover, the

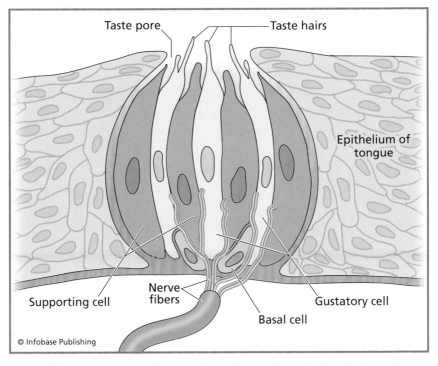

Figure 3.2   Taste buds are made up of supporting cells, basal cells, and gustatory cells.

connection between the nerve fibers and old gustatory cells must be disrupted, and new synapses formed. Finally, **supporting cells**, which are found between gustatory cells, provide support to the taste buds. They are the majority cell type and help insulate sensory cells. Although supporting cells are shaped like gustatory cells, they lack taste hairs.

TASTE SENSATIONS

When an individual's taste is tested with pure chemicals, five distinct sensations or qualities are detected: sweet, salty, sour, bitter, and umami. A sweet taste is produced by many organic compounds, especially sugars, as well as by some alcohols and amino acids. Unfortunately, the salts in lead paint have a sweet taste, which explains why young children are sometimes tempted to eat peeling paint. Sweetness is associated with foods high in caloric value and helps satisfy our need for carbohydrates and some amino acids. Saccharin, an artificial sweetener, tastes about 700 times sweeter than sucrose (table sugar), which is why it provides the sensation of sweetness without calories. Fructose (fruit sugar) also tastes sweeter than sucrose and is often added to soft drinks to enhance their sweetness. Interestingly, many plants have evolved sweet nectar and fruits to entice animals to eat them, thereby dispersing their pollen and seeds.

Sour taste is usually associated with acids, especially with hydrogen ions (H^+) in solution. Citrus fruits often taste sour because they contain citric acid, which releases H^+ when dissolved in saliva. Taste for sour is beneficial because many sour, naturally acidic foods, such as citrus fruits, are excellent sources of vitamins and minerals.

Salty sensations are produced by metal ions, such as sodium (Na^+) and potassium (K^+). These ions are important electrolytes for body fluids, which explains why there is value in our ability to taste them.

Spoiled foods, alkaloids (such as caffeine, nicotine, quinine, and morphine), and some nonalkaloids (like aspirin) have a bitter taste. It is advantageous for us to be able to taste bitter items because these substances are often poisonous. In fact, a bitter sensation often makes us reject the item we ingested. However, many vegetables, such as broccoli and tofu, contain bitter chemicals that act as anticancer agents. A number of people develop a taste for these and other bitter foods, such as olives and quinine water. Interestingly, although fruits and nectar are sweet, the leaves of many plants contain bitter, toxic alkaloids. This makes sense because it is not advantageous for plants to have their leaves eaten.

A fifth sensation, umami (a Japanese word for "delicious"), was recently discovered and is now considered a primary taste sensation. Umami is a pleasant taste elicited by amino acids, such as glutamate and aspartate, and by some small peptides and nucleotides. It is responsible for the "beef taste" of steak or beef broth. Umami also enhances other taste qualities, which is why monosodium glutamate (MSG), with its umami taste, is often used as a food additive or flavor enhancer. However, glutamate also is an excitatory neurotransmitter in the central nervous system. For this reason, those people who are sensitive to MSG respond by getting headaches and feeling flushed and dizzy when they eat it. Because MSG has often been used in Chinese foods, sensitivity to it is sometimes called "Chinese restaurant syndrome."

In addition to the five basic qualities of taste described above, there are two accessory taste qualities: alkaline and metallic. An alkaline (soapy) sensation is produced by stimulation with potassium carbonate (potash), and some metals and metal salts have a specific metallic taste. Finally, although most people say that water has no taste, there are, in fact, water taste receptors in the pharynx. Signals from these receptors are processed by the hypothalamus of the brain and, in turn, affect body water balance and the regulation of blood volume.

SENSORY MAP OF THE TONGUE

There are no visible structural differences between taste buds in different areas of the tongue. However, sensory maps of the tongue developed in the early 20th century (as a result of misinterpreted data reported in the late 1800s) have been commonly reproduced in textbooks. These maps indicate that certain regions of the tongue are more sensitive to one kind of taste than to others. For instance, the tip of the tongue is noted for being most sensitive to sweet tastes, whereas the sides of the tongue are more sensitive to salty and sour tastes. The back of the tongue is said to be especially sensitive to bitter substances, which tend to trigger a rejection response, such as gagging, to protect against the ingestion of poisons and toxins. In fact, the threshold for bitter taste is the lowest of all tastes, meaning that we can taste lower concentrations of alkaloids than of sugars, acids, and salts. However, it should be noted that although taste maps are common in scientific literature, in reality, all taste buds respond to all taste qualities, and all primary tastes can be detected by all areas of the tongue that contain taste buds. In fact, there is no evidence that specific taste sensitivities of certain tongue areas affect the way we perceive different taste qualities.

Interestingly, mixing different qualities of tastes is not like mixing different colors of paint or light. For instance, when blue and yellow paints are mixed, the color green is produced, and there is no longer any indication of the two original colors. In contrast, when different tastes are mixed, each individual taste can still be detected. Lemonade, for example, simultaneously tastes both sweet and sour because it contains sugar and citric acid. Our ability to discriminate and combine different tastes is the essence of fine cooking, and chefs mix various combinations of spices to bring out different taste sensations.

People differ in how sensitive they are to taste. Some aspects of these individual differences can be inherited. For instance, students in a biology class may test their taste sensitivity with paper strips containing phenylthiourea (also known as phenylthiocarbamide or PTC). It turns out that approximately 70% of Caucasians can taste PTC (this ability is inherited as a dominant trait), whereas the other 30% are unable to detect it (this is inherited as a recessive trait). In addition, there are age-related changes in taste discrimination. For instance, the number of taste buds decreases around the age of 50; therefore, so does the sense of taste. It has been estimated that most humans are born with about 10,000 taste buds but may die with as few as 2,000 to 4,000. This helps explain, in part, why elderly people may find some foods bland and unappetizing, whereas children may find the same foods too spicy or pungent.

Finally, there can be functional problems that interfere with taste. Many of these disturbances result from diseases, such as brain tumors. For instance, **hypogeusia** is a condition where the threshold (minimum concentration) for taste perception is above the normal range. It is harder for people with this condition to taste substances than it is for most

DID YOU KNOW?

While eating food, the mouth is exposed to a number of different kinds of stimuli. For instance, because the mouth is in direct communication with the nose, volatile substances readily go from the mouth to odor receptors in the nose and give us the sensation of smell. In fact, much of what we perceive as taste involves the sense of smell. This helps explain why food tastes bland when your nose is stuffed-up from a cold or allergy. In addition, anyone who has walked into a coffeehouse knows that the aroma of coffee is quite strong. However, without the sense of smell, coffee would lose its appeal and would simply taste bitter. Similarly, without smell, cinnamon would have only a faintly sweet taste.

The mouth also contains thermoreceptors and mechanoreceptors, which are usually stimulated when we eat; in addition, nociceptors may be activated. In fact, "taste" is really a mixture of sensations: Odor, temperature, and texture, and possibly pain, are superimposed on the real taste sensations of sweet, salty, sour, bitter, and umami. For instance, thermoreceptors are involved when we say that lukewarm coffee tastes lousy, but piping hot coffee tastes great. Mechanoreceptors provide information about the texture of food, which is why some people say they don't like their green beans soft and mushy or don't like onions because they feel slimy. For some individuals, nociceptors need to be stimulated with chemicals found in hot chili peppers (e.g., capsaicin) for food to "taste" good.

people. Individuals with **ageusia** have no sense of taste at all. **Dysgeusia** refers to a distortion of taste in which the sensations experienced are usually unpleasant and do not correspond to the nature of a stimulus, or these sensations may occur without any stimulus at all.

SIGNAL TRANSDUCTION DURING TASTE

For a chemical to be tasted, it must first dissolve in saliva and enter a taste pore. Given that taste receptors respond to dissolved chemicals from a nearby source, they are also referred to as *contact chemoreceptors*. After contacting a taste hair, the chemical can set off an electrical change in the membrane of a sensory cell. This, in turn, causes a sensory cell to release specific chemicals that are stored in membranous sacs called *vesicles* found beneath the plasma membrane. These chemicals then bind to receptors on associated sensory nerve dendrites, which causes a change in the potential (voltage) across the nerve cell membrane. If this change is large enough, a signal is sent to the brain for interpretation.

There are still a number of unanswered questions concerning taste, especially with regard to relaying information to the central nervous system. For instance, taste signals sent to the brain do not represent a single taste modality. In other words, a single nerve leaving the tongue may send signals in response to both sour and salty tastes or both sour and bitter tastes. Because a single taste bud can respond to more than one kind of stimulant, it is unclear how distinct taste sensations are coded. It is possible that single nerve fibers from the tongue, even though they respond to more than one type of taste, have distinct preferences, with some responding best to sugar, others to salt, and others to acid. Perhaps these fibers serve as labeled lines that signal distinct taste sensations, or a perception of taste may occur only from the comparison of the activity of a large population of nerve fibers. The answers to these questions remain to be elucidated.

CONNECTIONS

The sense of taste (gustation) is controlled by chemorecep-tors that respond to chemicals dissolved in a watery solution on the tongue. Gustation is important because it provides information about the quality of the foods and liquids we consume. The sensory receptor organs for gustation are the taste buds, which are structures composed of specialized epithelial cells.

The tongue has epithelial projections or folds called lingual papillae, which are peglike bumps. There are four types of lingual papillae, which differ in distribution and structure; only three of them bear taste buds. Foliate papillae are arranged as closely packed folds along the back edges of the tongue. Fungiform papillae are mushroom-shaped and are the only papillae scattered over the entire surface of the tongue. They usually contain two to five taste buds located on the top surface. Circumvallate papillae are the largest in size; each contains about 250 taste buds. Filiform papillae are tiny bumps that cover the tongue. Although they are the most numerous papillae, they play no sensory role because they lack taste buds.

Taste buds are made up of 40 to 150 epithelial cells that are of three major types. Gustatory cells are slender cells that have taste hairs (microvilli). Water-soluble substances that reach the surface of the tongue can move through a taste pore into a fluid-filled space over the taste bud. A typical gustatory cell lives only about 7 to 10 days, and these cells are continu-ally replaced as nearby basal cells divide and turn into new sensory cells. Supporting cells, found between sensory cells, support the taste buds. These supporting cells are the most common cell type in taste buds. They lack taste hairs and help insulate gustatory cells.

Humans are able to detect five distinct taste sensations or qualities: sweet, salty, sour, bitter, and umami. A sweet taste is produced by many organic compounds, especially sugars

(continues)

(continued)

and some amino acids. Sour is associated with acids, particularly with hydrogen ions (H^+). Salty sensations are produced by metal ions, such as sodium (Na^+) and potassium (K^+). Bitter tastes come from spoiled foods, alkaloids, and some non-alkaloids (such as aspirin). A fifth sensation, umami, is a pleasant taste produced by amino acids, such as glutamate and aspartate. It is responsible for the "beef" taste of steak.

Sensory maps of the tongue indicate that there are slight regional differences in primary sensitivity. The tip of the tongue is most sensitive to sweet tastes, whereas the sides of the tongue are more sensitive to salty and sour tastes, and the back of the tongue is especially sensitive to bitter substances. Although taste maps are common in scientific literature, it is important to remember that all taste buds respond to most, if not all, taste qualities.

The perception of taste is a sensation that depends on many factors, including the sense of smell (chemoreceptors), as well as input from thermoreceptors, mechanoreceptors, and nociceptors.

4

Sense of Smell

Olfaction, THE SENSE OF SMELL, ORIGINATES WITH chemoreceptors that respond to chemicals in solution. However, unlike the chemoreceptors for taste, olfactory receptors are adapted to respond to external chemicals from a distant source. For this reason, they are also referred to as *distance chemoreceptors*, and they have a much lower threshold (are more sensitive) than contact chemoreceptors. Although modest compared to the noses of many other animals (dogs can sense odors at concentrations more than a million times lower than people), the human nose can discriminate among thousands of different odor substances; most people can tell the difference between 2,000 to 4,000 odors, and some can detect up to 10,000 odors. For instance, if you were blindfolded, you could likely tell the difference between your best friend's house and other homes simply by the odors. Some individuals, such as professional wine tasters and tea tasters, make a living through the use of their sense of smell.

Olfaction is important because it provides information about the quality of the air we breathe. For example, smelling a noxious gas, such as ammonia, will cause a reflex that interrupts our breathing. In addition, we may receive subtle cues about another person's mood by the odors he or she gives off. In fact, perfume manufacturers take advantage of some of these odors. Interestingly, on average, women tend to be more sensitive to odors than men and are more sensitive to certain odors near the time of ovulation compared with other phases of their menstrual cycle.

LOCATION OF OLFACTORY RECEPTORS

The **nasal cavity**, the space between the roof of the mouth and the floor of the skull, is divided into two spaces, left and right, by a partition called the **nasal septum**. The surface area of each space is enlarged by folds that form ridges called **conchae**. The adult human has three conchae, arranged one on top of the other on each side of the nasal septum. The entire nasal cavity is lined with a mucous membrane that includes epithelial

DOGS SENSE HUMAN HEALTH

Because dogs can identify chemical traces in the range of parts per trillion, scientists have been testing whether canines can detect cancer in its early stages. For instance, studies have shown that dogs can detect skin cancer (melanomas) by sniffing skin lesions. A recent scientific study indicates that dogs can detect whether someone has cancer just by sniffing that person's breath. In fact, it was shown that after only a few weeks of training, ordinary household dogs learned to distinguish between breath samples of lung- and breast-cancer patients and healthy subjects. Apparently, cancer patients exhale volatile biochemical markers in their breath that are not found in healthy individuals. These markers can be detected by a dog's amazing sense of smell. Given that early detection of cancers improves survival chances, it is possible that dogs may become a diagnostic tool in early screening. Related to this, some researchers wonder whether dogs may be able to detect prostate cancer by smelling a patient's urine.

cells with many hairlike structures (cilia) and goblet cells, which produce mucus. However, the nasal receptor cells, called **olfactory cells**, are found only in a small area called the **olfactory region**, which is a yellow-tinged patch about 2 to 4 square centimeters (0.3 to 0.6 in.^{2}) in humans (and about 18 cm^2 (2.8 in.^{2}) in dogs). It contains 10 to 20 million cells (compared to 200 million in canines). The olfactory region is located over all of the upper concha and as islands on the middle concha. This region also contains supporting cells and basal cells similar to those found in taste buds. However, unlike taste cells, which are epithelial cells, olfactory cells are actual neurons (nerve cells).

The olfactory epithelium is actually not in the best position for detecting odors because the air that enters the nasal cavity has to make a hairpin turn to stimulate the receptors before going into the respiratory passage below. In fact, a normal, relaxed inhalation carries about 2% of the air breathed in to the olfactory regions. However, sniffing, which draws air upward across the olfactory epithelium, increases the sense of smell.

In the human fetus, the mucous membrane on the nasal septum contains closed tubules that appear to lead to nowhere. These structures form what is left of the *vomeronasal organ*, which is an olfactory organ that plays an important role in many amphibians, reptiles, and mammals other than humans. For instance, when a snake sticks out its forked tongue, it is picking up chemicals in the air, which it then touches to its vomeronasal organ. The function of the vomeronasal organ in humans is still under debate.

STRUCTURE OF THE OLFACTORY REGION

The **olfactory epithelium** contains olfactory cells, basal cells, and supporting cells (Figure 4.1). The supporting cells contain a yellow-brown pigment that gives the olfactory epithelium a yellowish hue. As with taste buds, the basal cells replace other cell types in the olfactory epithelium as they die off. The olfactory cells, which are shaped like bowling pins,

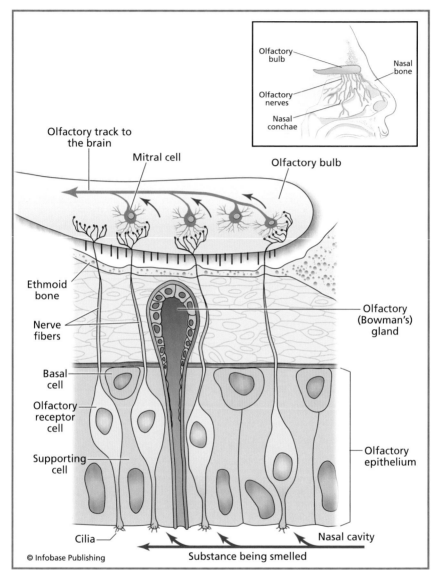

Olfactory bulb

Nasal bone

Olfactory nerves

Nasal conchae

Olfactory track to the brain

Mitral cell

Olfactory bulb

Ethmoid bone

Nerve fibers

Olfactory (Bowman's) gland

Basal cell

Olfactory receptor cell

Supporting cell

Olfactory epithelium

Cilia

Nasal cavity

© Infobase Publishing

Substance being smelled

Figure 4.1   The olfactory epithelium is located on the roof of the nasal cavity. When you inhale odorant molecules, they dissolve in the fluid on the olfactory epithelium and bind to receptors on the cilia of the olfactory receptor cells.

pins, are unique in that they are the only neurons in the body that are directly exposed to the external environment. They are also one of the few types of neurons that are continually replaced throughout life. In fact, their typical life span is about 60 days, after which they are replaced by the continuous division and differentiation of basal cells.

The olfactory cells have 10 to 20 long, hairlike structures called *cilia* at their apical (outward-facing) poles. These **olfactory cilia** give the olfactory epithelium more surface area with which to detect smells. Amazingly, the exposed surface area generated by olfactory cilia actually approaches that of the entire body surface area, about 2 square meters (3,100 in.[2]).

The olfactory cilia are typically covered by a coat of mucus, which dissolves odor-causing substances in the air. The molecules of an odorant must go through part of this mucus layer before they get to the olfactory cilia. The mucus is produced by supporting cells of the olfactory epithelium and by **olfactory glands** in the connective tissue underneath. The basal end of each olfactory cell tapers to become an axon. An **axon** is the single, long, fiberlike extension of a nerve cell that passes electrical signals called **action potentials** to other neurons or muscles. The axons of the olfactory cells leave the nasal cavity through pores in part of the bone of the skull. Together, these axons are called the **olfactory nerve**.

ODOR SENSATIONS

Although the basic tastes have been divided into five types, efforts to identify primary odors have been inconclusive and remain controversial. For practical purposes, we can describe a series of qualities or odor classes. A few of these primary odors (and the chemicals that produce them) include flowery (beta-phenylethyl alcohol), etheric (benzylacetate), musky (ring ketones), camphorous (camphor), sweaty (butyric acid), rotten (hydrogen sulfide), and pungent (formic acid). It should be noted, however, that substances that are similar chemically may fall into different odor classes, and members of a single odor class can have very different chemical structures.

Some studies suggest that there are at least 1,000 "odor genes." Each gene apparently codes for a unique odor receptor molecule. However, given the large number of odors that we can detect, it is unlikely that an olfactory cell has a specific receptor molecule for each and every odor substance. Instead, it seems more likely that each receptor molecule responds to a number of different odors, and each odor substance may bind

DID YOU KNOW?

Pheromones are chemicals that are somewhat similar to hormones, but instead of being transported by the bloodstream, they move through the air from one person to another, thereby allowing one individual to influence the physiology of another. For example, pheromones in a person's bodily secretions may affect the sexual physiology of others. A woman's sweat appears to influence the timing of other women's menstrual cycles. This may explain the so-called "dormitory effect," in which women who live together tend to get their menstrual periods around the same time. In addition, the presence of women makes a man's beard grow faster, and the presence of men seems to influence the timing of female ovulation. When a woman is ovulating or close to ovulation, her vaginal secretions contain pheromones that have been shown to raise men's testosterone levels.

An interesting study was conducted to find out whether a woman's choice of a mate might be influenced by smell. A group of men were asked to wear a T-shirt for several days in a row. The shirts were then laid out, one next to the other. Without knowing who had worn which shirt, women were asked to tell which shirts smelled pleasant or unpleasant. Interestingly, the shirts that the women said had a pleasing odor had been worn by men who had an HLA (human leukocyte antigen) complex that was different from that of the woman who had smelled them. In contrast, the shirts each woman found unpleasant to smell had been worn by men with an HLA complex similar to her own. It turns out that mates who have different HLA complexes may increase the chances that their offspring will have stronger immune systems. Thus, from an evolutionary point of view, there might be an overall survival advantage for women to be influenced by odor when selecting their mates.

to several different receptors. Evidence that receptor molecules interact with more than one odor substance can be seen in the phenomenon of partial **anosmia**, a condition in which a person cannot smell a specific odor or odors. It turns out that about 0.5% of the people in Europe have symptoms of partial anosmia. When these people try to smell different odors, they cannot detect a small number of substances that smell similar (e.g., certain musky odors). Thus, the existence of partial anosmia indicates that the number of odor qualities that we can detect is limited to some extent and that receptor molecules can be stimulated by more than one odor substance.

Another problem with defining odor qualities is that it is hard to determine which properties are needed to give a substance an odor. For instance, in order for us to smell something, it must be volatile (able to evaporate and exist as a gas) and be carried by inhaled air into the nasal cavity. In addition, the substance must dissolve in the fluid that coats the olfactory epithelium. However, the intensity of smells is not just related to its volatility. For instance, water is highly volatile (evaporates easily), but has virtually no odor. In contrast,

DID YOU KNOW?

Motile cilia (those that are capable of movement) in the part of the nasal cavity that handles breathing control the flow of mucus that is produced by supporting cells and olfactory glands. Cilia are sensitive to temperature. When it gets too cold, they become temporarily paralyzed. This explains why your nose "runs" when you inhale outside air on a cold winter's day—the mucus is still being produced, but the cilia cannot move it towards your pharynx. This is also why your nose stops running soon after you go indoors. The cilia of the respiratory tract are also paralyzed by cigarette smoke, which is why many smokers may develop a chronic cough. The cough is the body's way of trying to clear mucus that gets trapped in the respiratory tree.

musk, found in animal scent glands, has a very distinctive odor, but is not very volatile. In general, odorants are small organic molecules, and the strongest smells usually go along with molecules that are very soluble in both water and lipids. One example is butyl mercaptan, which has a very low detection threshold (very low concentrations elicit a sensation of smell). This chemical gives off an unpleasant, rotten, garlicky smell, which is why it is often added to natural gas to make gas leaks easier to detect.

TRANSDUCTION DURING SMELL

Dissolved chemicals (odorants) stimulate olfactory receptors by binding to a receptor protein or proteins in the cilia of olfactory cells. This, in turn, activates **adenylate cyclase**, an enzyme that turns adenosine triphosphate (ATP) into **cyclic adenosine monophosphate** (**cAMP**). The cAMP molecules interact with sodium channels in the olfactory cell membrane, causing them to open. Open sodium channels allow positively charged sodium ions (Na^+) to flow inward, which depolarizes the cell membrane. That is, it gives the inside of the cell a less negative charge. A sufficiently large depolarization triggers an action potential in the nerve axon, which goes to the end of the olfactory tract, the **olfactory bulb** of the brain. Some odors, including ammonia, menthol, chlorine,

DID YOU KNOW?

Although olfactory receptors are constantly replaced, the total number of receptors we have declines as we age, and our remaining receptors become less sensitive. As a result, older people often have difficulty detecting odors in low concentrations. This decrease in the number of receptors and their sensitivity helps explain why your grandmother may apply too much perfume or your grandfather may overdo his application of aftershave.

and hot peppers, stimulate nociceptors rather than olfactory cells. The "smelling salts" used to help revive an unconscious person also stimulate nociceptors.

THE OLFACTORY PATHWAY

Olfactory nerve fibers pass through part of the skull and enter a pair of olfactory bulbs beneath the frontal lobes of the brain. There, the nerves connect with neurons called **mitral cells** and form complex structures called **glomeruli** (singular, *glomerulus*). Each glomerulus receives only one type of odor signal, and different odors, which would excite a variety of receptor types, likely activate different glomeruli. The mitral cells serve to refine and amplify signals that come from olfactory nerves and then send those signals to other areas of the brain via **olfactory tracts** (the axons of mitral cells). Although as few as four molecules of an odorous substance can activate an olfactory receptor and its associated nerve fibers, we may not necessarily be aware of the stimulus. This is because olfactory bulbs also house **granule cells**, which can inhibit the activity of mitral cells. When this happens, only highly excitatory olfactory impulses are transmitted from the glomeruli. This inhibition helps cause olfactory **adaptation**, a decrease in responsiveness during continued stimulation, and explains why we may become unaware of our own body odor or a bread baking in a kitchen. In fact, olfactory receptors adapt very little to a persistent stimulus, and it is, instead, adaptation in the central nervous system that makes us quickly lose awareness of one smell while remaining sensitive to others.

When mitral cells are activated, nerve impulses flow from the olfactory bulbs to two main destinations via the olfactory tracts. Some signals go through a sorting center in the brain, called the **thalamus**, to the cerebral cortex, where smells are consciously interpreted and identified. Olfactory signals also are sent to other regions of the brain, which include the **amygdala** and **hypothalamus**, and other parts of the **limbic system** (Figure 4.2). The limbic system plays an important role in

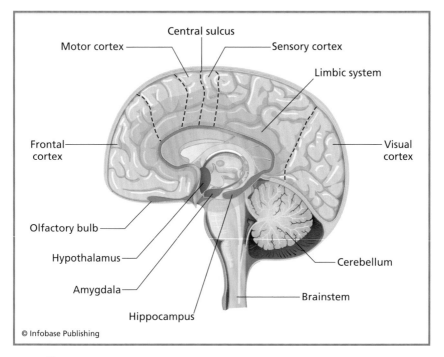

Central sulcus
Motor cortex
Sensory cortex
Limbic system
Frontal cortex
Visual cortex
Olfactory bulb
Hypothalamus
Amygdala
Cerebellum
Brainstem
Hippocampus

© Infobase Publishing

Figure 4.2 This view of the human brain shows the structures that make up the limbic system, a portion of the brain that is important for feeling and interpreting emotions. The amygdala recognizes angry or fearful facial expressions, assesses danger, and elicits an appropriate response. Interestingly, smell signals go to the limbic system, where the odors may cause specific emotional responses and memories.

feeling emotions. The hypothalamus contains centers that control the autonomic (unconscious) functions of the body. Thus, signals generated by smell can trigger strong emotional and physical reactions by influencing the limbic system, even if we are not consciously aware of an odor. For example, the smell of certain foods can increase salivation and stimulate the digestive tract. The perfume industry expends considerable effort trying to develop odors that trigger sexual responses. In contrast, odors associated with unpleasant items, such as raw sewage, a skunk, or decaying flesh, can trigger a **fight-or-flight response** and can even make us vomit. In addition, the cerebral cortex sends its own signals to the olfactory bulbs. These brain-generated signals can change the quality and significance of odors under different conditions. For instance, food may smell more appealing when you are hungry and may seem less appetizing after a large meal.

CONNECTIONS

The sense of smell (olfaction) is regulated by chemoreceptors that allow us to detect thousands of different odor substances. The nasal cavity is divided into two spaces by a partition called the nasal septum. The surface area of each space is enlarged by folds that form ridges called conchae. Adult humans have three conchae. The entire nasal cavity is lined with a mucous membrane that includes ciliated epithelial cells and mucus-producing goblet cells. Olfactory cells exist only in a small area called the olfactory region. This area also contains supporting cells and basal cells, which are similar to those in taste buds. However, unlike taste cells, which are epithelial cells, olfactory cells are neurons.

Olfactory cells undergo regular turnover throughout life. These cells have a life span of about 60 days, after which they are replaced by the new cells produced by continuous division and differentiation of basal cells. Olfactory cells have 10 to 20 long cilia at their apical poles. These olfactory cilia increase the amount of surface area available to receive odors. The olfactory cilia are typically covered by a coat of mucus, which helps dissolve airborne substances. The basal end of each olfactory cell tapers to become an axon, which leaves the nasal cavity through pores in the skull.

Efforts to identify primary odors have been inconclusive and controversial. Some studies suggest that there are at least 1,000 "odor genes." In general, odorants (dissolved chemicals) are small organic molecules, and the strongest smells are often associated with molecules that are easily dissolved in both water and lipids.

(continues)

(continued)

Odorant molecules stimulate olfactory receptors by binding to a receptor protein in the cilia of olfactory cells. This, in turn, activates adenylate cyclase, an enzyme that converts ATP to cyclic AMP (cAMP). The cAMP molecules stimulate sodium channels, which depolarize the membrane. A large enough depolarization fires an action potential (impulse) in the nerve axon, which will be sent to the olfactory bulb of the brain. Some odors activate nociceptors rather than olfactory cells.

Olfactory nerve fibers pass through pores in the skull and enter a pair of olfactory bulbs. There, the nerves connect with mitral cells and form complex structures called glomeruli. The mitral cells refine and amplify smell signals and then relay them other areas of the brain. Granule cells inhibit the activity of mitral cells, so only highly excitatory olfactory impulses are transmitted from the glomeruli. This inhibition contributes to the mechanisms of olfactory adaptation. When mitral cells are activated, nerve impulses flow from the olfactory bulbs to the cerebral cortex, where smells are consciously interpreted and identified. Olfactory signals also are sent to the amygdala, hypothalamus, and other parts of the limbic system. These signals can trigger strong emotional and physical reactions.

5

Accessory Structures of the Eye

THE ADULT EYE (FIGURE 5.1) IS A SPHERE WITH A DIAMETER OF about 2.5 cm (1 in.). Only the front one-sixth of its surface is visible. The rest is enclosed and protected by a cushion of fat and the walls of the **orbit** (the cavity in the frontal bone of the skull). The eye is a complex structure, and only a small part of its tissues are directly involved with **photoreception**, the conversion of light energy into chemical energy. Photoreception can lead to **vision**, the perception of objects in the environment by means of the light they emit or reflect. In fact, vision is the dominant sense for human beings; we rely on vision more than any other special sense. This is indicated by the fact that 70% of all the sensory receptors in our body are found in the eyes, and almost half of the cerebral cortex is involved with some aspect of processing vision.

The accessory structures of the eye include the eyebrows, eyelids, conjunctiva (outer surface of the eyeball), lacrimal apparatus (the structures that produce and secrete tears), and the extrinsic eye muscles.

EYEBROWS

The **eyebrows** are made up of short, coarse hairs that lie on the exterior ridges of the skull above the eye. Although they

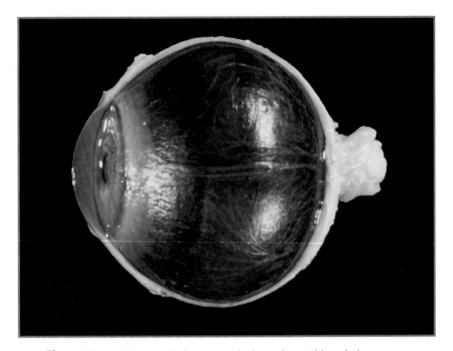

Figure 5.1   A side view of a human eye is shown here. Although the eye is about 2.5 cm (1 in.) in diameter, we can see only about one-sixth of its surface under normal conditions.

are not directly involved with the visual process, they do serve important functions that help with vision. For instance, they can protect the eyes against glare, shade the eyes from sunlight, and prevent perspiration from running down the forehead into the eyes. They also have functions that are not related to vision; they can be used, for example, to enhance facial expressions, which is important in nonverbal communication. The eyebrows have special muscles that let them move both up and down and from side to side.

EYELIDS

The **eyelid** is a thin, movable fold of skin over each eye. It protects the eyes by preventing foreign objects and excessively bright light from reaching the eyeballs. It also keeps visual stimuli from disturbing us while we sleep. In addition, the eyelids act like miniature windshield wipers, sweeping foreign material from the eye surface. Blinking, which takes place about every 3 to 7 seconds, keeps the surface of the eye free from dust and other debris. It also keeps the eye surface moist and lubricated with secretions, such as oil, mucus, and saline solution.

The free margins of the upper and lower eyelids are separated by the **palpebral fissure** and meet at the corners, which are called the **medial** and **lateral commissures.** In most

DID YOU KNOW?

Light is a form of **electromagnetic energy** that travels through space as waves. Vision is well adapted for wavelengths of light within what we call the visible spectrum (roughly 400 to 700 nanometers [nm]) but not beyond. (A nanometer is one-billionth of a meter, and a meter is about 39 inches long.) Why is this? In part, it is because most solar radiation that reaches the surface of the Earth falls within this range. Radiation of shorter wavelengths, such as ultraviolet (UV) light, is absorbed by the atmosphere's ozone layer. Radiation of longer wavelengths, such as infrared, is filtered out of the atmosphere by carbon dioxide and water vapor. However, there also is a physiological explanation. To stimulate a receptor, light must produce a **photochemical reaction** in which the chemical structure of a molecule changes through its interaction with light energy. Electromagnetic radiation with a wavelength greater than 750 nm does not have enough energy to activate the visual process; it may feel warm (like the infrared radiation of a heat lamp), but it usually does not cause a chemical reaction. In contrast, radiation with a wavelength less than 400 nm has so much energy that it can kill cells. This is why ultraviolet radiation can be useful for sterilizing instruments, but it has too much energy for the biochemical process of vision. Nonetheless, some animals can detect radiation slightly beyond the range visible to humans. For instance, certain insects can see objects illuminated in the ultraviolet range that is invisible to mammals.

Asian people, a vertical fold of skin called the epicanthal fold commonly appears on both sides of the nose and sometimes covers the medial commissure. The eyelid itself is composed largely of muscles, called the orbicularis oculi and levator palpebrae superiorus, that are covered with skin. When the orbicularis oculi contracts, the eye closes. The upper eyelid raises when the levator muscle contracts. The eyelid also has a supportive, fibrous, thick connective tissue sheet along the margin of the eyelid, called the **tarsal plate.** This structure holds the eyelid muscles in place.

Eyelashes are sturdy hairs coming out of the margins of the eyelids that help keep foreign matter and insects from reaching the surface of the eye. Touching the eyelashes stimulates hair receptors and causes us to blink.

The eyelids have several types of glands. The medial commissure contains the **lacrimal caruncle,** a soft tissue mass that contains sebaceous (secreting a fatty lubricant) and sweat glands. Its thick, whitish, oily secretion sometimes collects at the medial commissure, especially during sleep. (It is sometimes called the "sandman's eye sand.") Along the inner margin of the eyelids are 20 to 25 modified sebaceous glands called **Meibomian glands**. These glands have ducts that open at the eyelid edge just behind the eyelashes. They secrete a lipid-rich product that moistens the eyelids and helps keep them from sticking together. This secretion also keeps tears from evaporating off the surface of the eye. Associated with the eyelash follicles are a number of smaller, more typical sebaceous glands, called the **glands of Zeis.** In addition, modified sweat glands known as *ciliary glands* lie between the eyelash hair follicles. Unfortunately, the glands of the eye can suffer from occasional infection by bacteria, which can form a **sty**—a painful, localized swelling, something like a pimple on the eyelid.

CONJUNCTIVA

The **conjunctiva** (literally meaning "joined together") is an epithelium that covers the inner surfaces of the eyelids (palpebral conjunctiva) and the outer surface of the eye (ocular conjunctiva), excluding the cornea (the clear tissue over the pupil and iris). It is a mucous membrane covered by a special tissue of stratified squamous epithelium. Its main function is to secrete a thin film of mucus that prevents the eyeball from drying out. The conjunctiva is highly sensitive to touch because it is filled with nerves. It also has many blood vessels. When these blood vessels are dilated, the eyes look "bloodshot." Damage or irritation to the conjunctiva can cause **conjunctivitis,** or "pinkeye." The most obvious symptom of conjunctivitis is reddening caused by dilation of the blood vessels beneath the epithelium. Conjunctivitis may be caused by infection with bacteria or viruses, and it is highly contagious. It also may result from physical or chemical irritation of the surface of the conjunctiva.

LACRIMAL APPARATUS

A constant flow of tears keeps the conjunctival surfaces moist and clean. The **lacrimal apparatus** is made up of several structures that produce, distribute, and remove tears. It includes the lacrimal gland with its associated ducts, lacrimal canals, a lacrimal sac, and a nasolacrimal duct (Figure 5.2).

DID YOU KNOW?

Many animals, including reptiles, birds, and some mammals, have an additional eyelid called the nictitating membrane. This clear membrane is part of the conjunctiva and can be drawn across the eyeball for protection from debris and dryness, similar to regular eyelids. For instance, sharks close the nictitating membrane to prevent their eyes from being poked by thrashing prey, and birds flying at high speeds will close this membrane to keep their eyes moist without loss of vision. Similarly, predators use the nictitating membrane to avoid blinking while looking for fast moving prey.

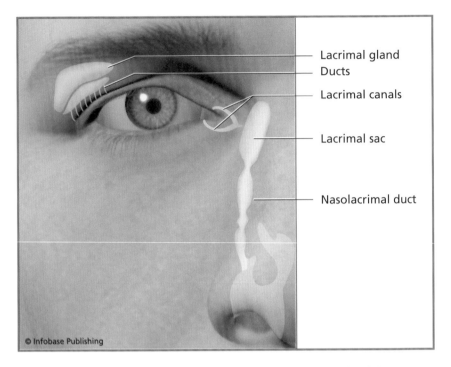

Figure 5.2   The lacrimal apparatus includes the lacrimal gland and the ducts that drain lacrimal secretions (tears) into the nasal cavity. Lacrimal fluid includes mucus, antibodies, and lysozyme. These ingredients allow tears to moisten, cleanse, and protect the surface of the eye.

The **lacrimal gland** is about the size and shape of an almond and is nestled in a shallow fossa (depression) of the frontal bone of the skull, above the lateral end of the eye (the side farthest from the nose). It is visible through the conjunctiva when the eyelid is turned inside out. The lacrimal gland releases about 1 milliliter (0.03 ounces) per day of a dilute saline solution called **lacrimal secretion**, commonly known as tears. Tears drain to the surface of the conjunctiva through 12 or so short ducts. Lacrimal secretion contains water, salts, mucus, antibodies, and **lysozyme**, an enzyme that has antibacterial properties. Thus, tears reduce friction, remove debris, help prevent bacterial infection, and bring nutrients and oxygen to the conjunctiva.

DID YOU KNOW?

Because tears eventually drain into the nasal cavity, an abundance of tears from crying or watery eyes (like you may get with allergies) can result in a runny nose. Once the tears enter the nasal cavity, they normally flow back into the throat (through the action of cilia) and we swallow them. However, when we have a cold or allergy, the nasolacrimal ducts can become swollen and obstructed, which prevents tears from draining properly. This, in turn, makes tears overflow from the brim of the eye.

Once the lacrimal secretions have reached the eye surface, they mix with the products of accessory glands, such as the oily secretion of the Meibomian glands. Blinking sweeps tears across the eye surface, and they accumulate at the medial commissure, where they enter the **lacrimal canals** through two tiny

YOUR HEALTH: EYES OUT OF ALIGNMENT

If the movements of the external muscles of the two eyes are not perfectly coordinated, a person cannot properly focus images from each eye. In such cases, a person will usually see two images instead of one, a condition known as **diplopia** (double vision). This can result from paralysis or weakness of certain outer muscles; it can also occur temporarily when someone drinks large amounts of alcohol. In addition, a congenital (inherited) weakness of the external eye muscles may cause **strabismus**, an abnormal alignment of the eye that is sometimes called "wandering eye." In some instances, only the eye that the person can control is used for vision. When this is the case, the brain ignores input from the wandering eye, which can become functionally blind. Less severe cases of strabismus can be treated with eye exercises to strengthen weak muscles or by placing a patch over the stronger eye, which forces the person to use the weaker eye. In more serious cases, however, surgery may be needed to repair the eye muscle.

openings called **lacrimal puncta** (these are visible as two tiny dots on the medial margin of each eyelid). From the lacrimal canals, the tears drain into the **lacrimal sac** and then into the **nasolacrimal duct**, which delivers tears to the **inferior meatus** of the nasal cavity.

EXTRINSIC EYE MUSCLES

Six straplike **extrinsic eye muscles** control the movement of each eyeball. The six muscles attach directly to the external surface of the eyeball and to the walls of the orbit. These muscles allow the eyes to follow a moving object, help maintain the shape of the eyeball, and hold the eye within the orbit. The outer eye muscles are among the most precisely and rapidly controlled skeletal muscles in the body. This is because they have a low ratio of muscle fibers to nerves (about 23:1).

The outer eye muscles handle two basic types of eye movements: saccades and scanning. **Saccades** are small, jerky movements that quickly move the eye from one spot to another, allowing us to see an entire visual field in a short period of time. In contrast, **scanning movements** track an object that is moving; that is, they allow us to follow a particular object moving in our visual field or to maintain our gaze on a fixed object as we move our heads.

CONNECTIONS

The adult eye is a sphere that is enclosed and protected by a cushion of fat and by the walls of the orbit. Photoreception can lead to vision, the perception of objects in the environment by means of the light that they emit or reflect. Eyebrows are short, coarse hairs that lie on the outside ridges of the skull above the eye. They protect the eyes against glare, shade the eyes from sunlight, and keep perspiration from running down the forehead into the eyes.

The eyelids protect the eyes by blocking foreign objects and light that is too bright. Blinking every three to seven seconds keeps the surface of the eye free from dust and other debris and also keeps the eye surface moist and lubricated with secretions (like oil, mucus, and saline solution).

The free margins of the upper and lower eyelids are separated by the palpebral fissure and meet at the corners, which are called the medial and lateral commissures. The eyelid also contains a sheet of supportive, fibrous, thick connective tissue along its margin, called the tarsal plate.

Several types of glands are associated with the eyelids. The medial commissure contains the lacrimal caruncle, a soft mass of tissue that contains sebaceous and sweat glands. Its thick, whitish, oily secretion sometimes collects at the medial commissure, especially during sleep. Along the inner margin of the eyelids are modified sebaceous glands called Meibomian glands, whose lipid-rich secretion lubricates the eyelids and helps keep them from sticking together.

The conjunctiva is an epithelium covering the inner surfaces of the eyelids and the outer surface of the eye. Its main function is to produce a thin mucous film that prevents the eyeball from drying out. The conjunctiva is highly sensitive to touch because it is richly packed with nerves. It is also supplied with many blood vessels. Damage, irritation, and infection of the conjunctiva can cause conjunctivitis.

A constant flow of tears keeps the conjunctival surfaces moist and clean. Lacrimal fluid contains water, salts, mucus, antibodies, and the enzyme lysozyme. Thus, tears reduce friction, remove debris, inhibit bacterial infection, and help bring nutrients and oxygen to the conjunctiva. The lacrimal apparatus consists of the lacrimal gland with its associated ducts, lacrimal canals, a lacrimal sac, and a nasolacrimal duct. The lacrimal gland continually releases a dilute saline solution called lacrimal secretion (tears). Blinking sweeps tears across the eye surface, and they accumulate at the medial commissure, where they enter the paired lacrimal canals via two tiny openings called lacrimal puncta. From the lacrimal canals, the tears drain into the lacrimal sac and

(continues)

(continued)

then into the nasolacrimal duct, which delivers tears to the nasal cavity.

The movement of each eyeball is controlled by six strap-like outer eye muscles that attach directly to the external surface of the eyeball and to the walls of the orbit. These muscles allow the eyes to follow a moving object help maintain the shape of the eyeball and hold it in place. The external eye muscles are responsible for two basic types of eye movements: saccades and scanning.

6

Structure of the Eye

EACH EYE IS A SLIGHTLY IRREGULAR HOLLOW SPHERE, A LITTLE smaller than a Ping-Pong ball. The wall of the eye contains three distinct layers, called tunics, and two cavities (Figure 6.1).

THE TUNICS

The outermost layer of the eye is called the **tunica fibrosa**. It is divided into two regions: the sclera and cornea. The tendonlike **sclera**, which is the white part of the eye, consists of dense, fibrous connective tissue perforated by blood vessels and nerves. It protects and shapes the eyeball and provides a sturdy site for the extrinsic eye muscles to anchor. At the rear, the sclera connects with the dura mater—a tough membrane that covers the brain.

In contrast to the sclera, the **cornea** forms a transparent region that admits light into the eye. This is accomplished by a highly organized arrangement of collagen (a type of protein) fibers that minimizes the scattering of light. Because it is important for the cornea to be transparent, it contains no blood vessels. Its superficial epithelial cells get oxygen and nutrients from the tears that flow across its surface. There are numerous nerve endings in the cornea, making it the most sensitive

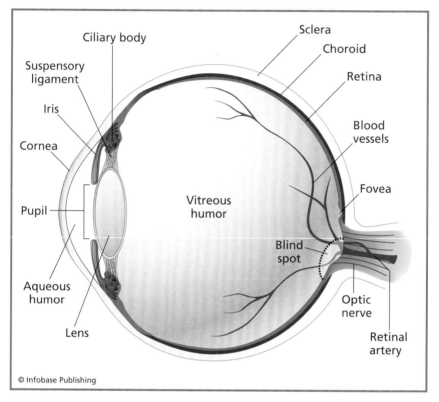

Figure 6.1 The cornea and lens focus light rays onto the fovea, the part of the retina that has the highest density of cones. When light is focused directly on the optic nerve (called the blind spot), the person cannot see the light. Because the two eyes have overlapping fields of view and because our brains are able to "fill in" missing details, we don't see any interruptions or gaps in the images around us.

portion of the eye. The cornea is also part of the light-bending apparatus of the eye. In fact, most of the bending of light (refraction) needed to focus an image on the retina actually occurs through the cornea.

The middle layer of the eye is called the **tunica vasculosa**, or *uvea* (which means "grape," since it resembles a peeled grape when it is dissected). It consists of three regions: the choroid, ciliary body, and iris. The **choroid** is a deeply pigmented membrane with many blood vessels. Its deep brown pigment (melanin) is produced by specialized cells called melanocytes and helps absorb light, preventing it from scattering and reflecting inside the eye. At the front of the eye, the choroid becomes the **ciliary body**. The ciliary body is made of interlacing bundles of smooth muscle, which are important for controlling the shape of the lens. The rear surface has radiating folds that contain capillaries (tiny blood vessels) that secrete the **aqueous humor**, the fluid that fills the anterior (front) chamber of the eye. The **iris**, the visible colored part of the eye, is an adjustable partition made of muscle and connective tissue that controls the diameter of the **pupil**, its central opening. The iris has two layers of smooth muscle that allow it to make the pupil narrow or widen. In close vision or in bright light, the pupil gets smaller. In contrast, the pupil dilates (widens) for distant vision or in dim light, allowing more light to enter the eye. The constriction of the pupil in response to light is called the **pupillary reflex**.

The **sensory tunic** is the innermost layer of the eye. It consists of an outer **pigmented layer,** which is only one cell thick, and a thicker, transparent inner layer called the **retina**. The pigmented epithelial cells in the outer layer, like those of the choroid, absorb light so that it does not scatter in the eye.

DID YOU KNOW?

A number of nocturnal animals have an extra layer of tissue in the eye called the tapetum lucidum (Latin phrase for "bright tapestry"), which is typically found immediately behind the retina. It essentially functions like a mirror, increasing retinal sensitivity in dim light by reflecting light back through the photoreceptor layer. This improves visual acuity in low-light conditions by providing rods with a second opportunity for stimulation. The presence of a tapetum lucidum can be observed at night when you see a pair of glowing animal eyes reflect back light, which can be blue, green, yellow, pink, or red in color.

This pigmented layer also stores vitamin A, which is needed by the retina's photoreceptor cells. The retina contains supporting cells and neurons that perform preliminary processing and integration of visual information. The neurons include **bipolar cells** and **ganglion cells**, where action potentials are generated (Figure 6.2). The **optic nerve**, which carries impulses for the sense of sight, exits the eye at the **optic disk** in the retina. This region is also called the **blind spot** because it has no photoreceptors. Thus, light focused on it cannot be seen. However, we are normally unaware of our blind spots because the visual cortex of the brain fills in the missing information. In

DID YOU KNOW?

The iris (from the Greek word for "rainbow") contains chromatophores, cells that produce melanin, a dark brown pigment. Eye color is determined by the amount and location of pigment produced, which is controlled by several different genes. At present, scientists are aware of three gene pairs that control human eye color (two pairs on chromosome 19 and one pair on chromosome 15). However, some inheritance patterns cannot be explained with these three gene pairs, suggesting that other genes that influence eye color remain to be discovered.

Essentially, if genetic makeup dictates the production of a high concentration of melanin in the iris, the person will have brown eyes. However, if the amount of pigment produced is small and only found on the rear surface of the iris, the shorter wavelengths of light can be scattered from the unpigmented cells, making the eyes look blue. This process is similar to the scattering of shorter wavelengths of light in the atmosphere, which gives the sky its blue color. Presumably, intermediate amounts of melanin produce different shades of brown, as well as gray, green, or hazel eyes. Albinos have a genetic mutation in which they don't produce pigment in their irises or in their skin and hair. Without melanin, the blood vessels in the back of the eyes reflect light, making the eyes look pink.

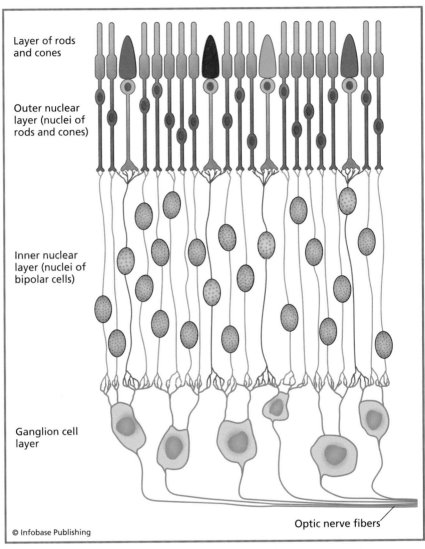

Layer of rods
and cones

Outer nuclear
layer (nuclei of
rods and cones)

Inner nuclear
layer (nuclei of
bipolar cells)

Ganglion cell
layer

Optic nerve fibers

Figure 6.2   The retina has three major kinds of neurons: rods and cones
(photoreceptors), bipolar cells, and ganglion cells. Bipolar and ganglion
cells fire action potentials that send the brain visual signals, while the
rods and cones help us to see in dim light and in color, respectively.

other words, the brain gives us an illusion of an uninterrupted
visual field. Finally, the retina contains blood vessels that
supply tissues lining the rear cavity. The central retinal artery

and vein pass through the center of the optic nerve and emerge on the surface of the optic disk.

PHOTORECEPTORS

There are two types of photoreceptors in the neural retina: rods and cones. The most numerous are the **rods**, which are used for vision in dim light and for peripheral vision (seeing from the sides of the eye). Rods do not discriminate between different colors of light, nor do they provide sharp images. That is why colors are indistinct and the edges of objects fuzzy when we see them in dim light or at the edges of our visual field. In contrast, **cones** work in bright light and give us clear and sharp color vision.

Rods and cones are not evenly distributed across the surface of the retina. Approximately 125 million rods form a broad band around the edge of the retina. Roughly 6 million cones span the rear surface of the retina surface. The **macula lutea** ("yellow spot") is a retinal region about 3 mm (0.12 in.) in diameter that contains mostly cones. Its central portion, the **fovea centralis**, has no rods and contains the highest concentration of cones. The fovea

YOUR HEALTH: CORNEAL INJURIES

Damage to the cornea can cause blindness even if the rest of the eye is perfectly normal. Although the cornea has some ability to repair itself, corneal injuries from severe scratches or other accidents must be treated quickly to prevent severe vision loss. Restoring vision after corneal scarring generally requires the replacement of the cornea through a transplant. In fact, corneal replacement is probably the most common form of transplant surgery. Because there are no blood vessels in the cornea to carry white blood cells, which attack foreign tissues, corneal transplants can be performed between unrelated individuals. Corneal grafts are taken from the eyes of donors who have recently died from illness or in accidents. The tissue should be removed within 5 hours of the donor's death for the best results.

DID YOU KNOW?

Cones cannot function in very dim light. For example, when you try to look at a dim star, you might be unable to see it when you look directly at it. However, the star often becomes more visible when you turn your head slightly and look a little to one side. This is because shifting your gaze moves the image of the star from the foveae of your eyes, where there is not enough light energy to stimulate cones, to the retinal periphery, where the light can stimulate rods, which have a relatively low threshold.

(plural, *foveae*) is where light is focused when we look directly at an object to give us the sharpest image. The fovea is about the size of the head of a pin (0.4 mm; 0.02 in.). As a result, to visually comprehend a scene that is rapidly changing, the eyes must flick rapidly back and forth so that the fovea receives images from different parts of the visual field.

YOUR HEALTH: RETINAL DETACHMENT

Although the two layers of the sensory tunic are close together, they are not fused. This makes the eye vulnerable to **retinal detachment**, a condition in which the retina separates from the pigmented layer, allowing the jellylike vitreous humor to seep between them. Retinal detachment can result from a sudden impact to the eye or when the head stops moving suddenly and is then jerked in the opposite direction (as can occur in a car accident or when bungee jumping). Some people describe the experience as a curtain being drawn across their eye. Others say they see sootlike spots or flashes of light. Retinal detachment deprives the retina of its nutrient source. Consequently, unless the two layers of the sensory tunic are reattached quickly, photoreceptors will degenerate and the person will become blind. The reattachment is generally performed by fusing the two layers together using a laser beam focused through the cornea, or by attaching a scleral buckle, a band that holds the retina in place.

CAVITIES OF THE EYE

The ciliary body and lens divide the interior of the eye into two cavities. The large **posterior** (rear) **cavity** contains a clear, gelatinous material called the **vitreous humor** (see Figure 6.1). Vitreous humor binds a large amount of water, allowing it to transmit light, hold the retina against the pigmented layer, and put pressure on the inside of the eye (called intraocular pressure), thereby helping to counteract the pulling force of the outer eye muscles. The vitreous humor forms before birth and lasts for an entire lifetime.

The smaller **anterior** (front) **cavity** is subdivided into two chambers. The **anterior chamber** extends from the cornea to the iris, and the **posterior chamber** lies between the iris and the ciliary body and lens. Both chambers are filled with aqueous humor, a clear fluid secreted by the ciliary body that is similar in composition to blood plasma. Aqueous humor is produced and drained continuously and is in constant motion. It flows from the

YOUR HEALTH: CATARACTS

How transparent the lens is depends on a precise combination of structural and biochemical characteristics. The lens can lose its transparency when this balance is disturbed, forming a **cataract**. A cataract is a clouding of the lens that makes vision appear distorted, as if you were looking through frosted glass. Cataracts may result from drug reactions, injuries, or radiation. However, the most common causes are age-related hardening and thickening of the lens or as a secondary consequence of diabetes mellitus. Heavy smoking and frequent exposure to ultraviolet radiation (like that of intense sunlight) increase the risk of developing cataracts. Ultimately, cataracts happen when the deeper lens fibers don't get enough nutrients. This leads to changes that result in the clumping of proteins. If the lens becomes sufficiently opaque, the person will become functionally blind. However, this condition can be treated surgically by removing the lens and replacing it with an artificial one. Then vision can be fine-tuned with eyeglasses or a contact lens.

posterior chamber through the pupil into the anterior chamber, where it is drained into the blood of the veins via the **canal of Schlemm**. Normally, the rate of removal balances the rate of secretion, about 1–2 microliters/minute (µl/min) (which converts to 0.02–0.04 drops of water/min), resulting in a constant intraocular pressure of 12–21 mm (0.5–0.8 in.) Hg. This, in turn, helps support the eyeball internally, much like air inside a balloon. The aqueous humor also provides nutrients and oxygen to the lens and cornea while carrying away their metabolic waste products.

THE LENS

The **lens** is a bioconvex, flexible structure that is suspended behind the pupil by a ring of fibers called the **suspensory ligament**, which attaches to the ciliary body. The main function of the lens is to focus images on the retinal photoreceptors. Like

YOUR HEALTH: GLAUCOMA

If aqueous humor begins to drain more slowly but is still produced at the same rate, the pressure within the eye may reach dangerously high levels, a condition known as **glaucoma**. Since the fibrous tunic cannot expand significantly, the increasing pressure will squeeze the retina and optic nerve. If untreated, the person will eventually go blind. Glaucoma affects about 2% of the population over age 35, and, unfortunately, there are usually no symptoms until damage has already occurred. Late signs include seeing halos around light or seeing flashes of light, as well as blurred vision.

Testing for glaucoma is a simple procedure. A puff of air is aimed at the sclera or the sclera is touched with a small probe, and then the amount of deformation that either causes is measured, giving a reading of the pressure inside the eye. Most eye-care specialists encourage people to have a glaucoma test done every year after the age of 40. People who have glaucoma usually give themselves eye drops that help drain the aqueous humor. A doctor may also perform corrective surgery, piercing the wall of the anterior chamber with a laser beam to increase drainage.

YOUR HEALTH: RETINOPATHY

The retina can be examined with an instrument called an ophthalmoscope, which both illuminates and magnifies an image. Eye examinations not only evaluate the eye's visual system but also allow doctors to check blood vessels for signs of hypertension (high blood pressure), diabetes mellitus (a disorder that affects how the body uses glucose), and atherosclerosis (hardening of the arteries). **Retinopathy** is a disease of the retina. Diabetic retinopathy develops in many individuals with diabetes mellitus. Diabetes can cause serious circulatory problems, including the degeneration and rupture of retinal blood vessels. As a consequence, a loss of clarity of vision (visual acuity) can occur over time as photoreceptors degenerate from oxygen starvation.

the cornea, it is avascular, meaning that it has no blood vessels (if it had blood vessels, it would not be transparent). The lens has two regions: the lens epithelium and the lens fibers. The lens epithelium is confined to the anterior surface. However, its cells differentiate into lens fibers that have no nuclei and few organelles (internal cell structures). These cells contain precisely folded transparent proteins. Because new lens fibers are always being added, the lens gets bigger as we age. Over time, the lens becomes less elastic, which gradually prevents it from being able to focus light. This condition, known as **presbyopia**, explains why people over the age of 40 commonly need reading glasses.

CONNECTIONS

Each eye is a sphere composed of three distinct layers, or tunics, and two cavities. The outermost layer, the tunica fibrosa, is divided into the sclera and the cornea. The tendon-like sclera consists of dense connective tissue perforated by blood vessels and nerves. It protects and shapes the eyeball, and provides a sturdy anchoring site for the extrinsic eye muscles. The cornea is modified to form a transparent region that admits light into the eye and is part of the light-bending apparatus of the eye.

The middle layer of the eye, the tunica vasculosa, consists of the choroid, ciliary body, and iris. The choroid is a highly vascular, deeply pigmented membrane. Its deep brown pigment (melanin) helps absorb light, preventing it from scattering and reflecting within the eye. At the front of the eye, the choroid becomes the ciliary body, which consists of interlacing smooth muscle bundles, which are important for controlling the shape of the lens. The posterior surface has radiating folds that contain capillaries, which secrete the aqueous humor. The iris, the visible colored part of the eye, controls the diameter of the pupil, its central opening. The iris has two layers of smooth muscle that allow it to adjust pupil size. The sensory tunic, the innermost layer of the eye, consists of an outer single-cell-thick pigmented layer and a thicker, transparent inner layer called the retina. Along with photoreceptors, the retina also contains supporting cells and neurons that handle the early processing of visual information. The optic nerve leaves the eye at the optic disk in the retina, also called the blind spot.

There are two types of photoreceptors in the retina: rods and cones. The rods function for vision in dim light and for peripheral vision and do not detect color. Cones operate in bright light and provide sharp color vision. The macula lutea is a retinal region that contains mostly cones. Its central portion, the fovea centralis, has no rods but contains the highest concentration of cones. The fovea is the place where light is focused when we look directly at an object to give us the sharpest image.

The ciliary body and lens divide the interior of the eye into a large posterior cavity, which contains a clear, gelatinous material called the vitreous humor and a smaller anterior cavity. The anterior cavity is subdivided into anterior and posterior chambers. Both chambers are filled with aqueous humor, a

(continues)

(continued)

clear fluid that is secreted by the ciliary body and flows from the posterior chamber through the pupil into the anterior chamber, where it is drained into the blood of the veins via the canal of Schlemm.

The lens is a bioconvex, flexible structure that is suspended behind the pupil by a ring of fibers called the suspensory ligament, which attaches to the ciliary body. The main function of the lens is to focus the images on the retinal photoreceptors. The lens fibers contain precisely folded transparent proteins. Because new lens fibers are continually added, the lens enlarges as we age and also becomes less elastic, which decreases its ability to focus light.

7

Sense of Sight

ALTHOUGH PHOTORECEPTION DEPENDS ON THE STIMULATION of photoreceptors, the visual process also requires a mechanism for focusing light rays on the retina. In many respects, the image-focusing system of the eyes works on a principle similar to that of a camera. For instance, the adjustable iris of the eye, which is something like a camera's shutter, can change the amount of light that enters the eye by altering the diameter of the pupil. Behind the pupil is a lens, a structure designed to focus light on the retina in a manner similar to a camera lens focusing light on film. Thus, the retina, a structure that contains photoreceptors, can be compared to the film in a camera.

PROPERTIES OF LIGHT

Our eyes respond to a specific region of the **electromagnetic spectrum** called **visible light**, which has a wavelength range of about 400 to 700 nm (1 nm = 10^{-9} m). When visible light passes through a prism, a **spectrum** (band of colors) can be seen. In fact, a rainbow is a spectrum formed when lots of tiny water droplets act together as prisms in the atmosphere during a rain shower. Interestingly, light has both wavelike and particlelike properties. That is, although light travels in waves with wavelengths that can be measured, it is also made up of small packets of energy called **photons**. It is the energy of these photons that stimulate our visual system.

REFRACTION

In a vacuum, light rays travel in straight lines at very fast speeds—300,000 kilometers per second (roughly 186,000 miles/s). Although the speed of light is constant in a given medium, it changes when light passes from one medium into another with a different density. For this reason, light slows down slightly in air, water, and glass. In addition, these changes cause a bending, or **refraction**, of light when it meets the surface of a different medium at an oblique angle. Refraction can easily be demonstrated by placing a straw in a partially filled glass of water. The straw will appear to "break" at the place where the air meets the water. The **refractive index** of a medium measures how much it retards (and therefore bends) light rays relative to air.

FOCUSING OF LIGHT

The lens of the eye functions like a camera lens. It is **convex** in shape—that is, it is thickest in the middle. The shape of the lens allows it to bend light rays so they meet at a single spot on the retina called the **focal point**. The distance between the center of the lens and its focal point is the **focal distance**, or focal length. The focal length is determined by: (1) how far an object is from the lens, and (2) the shape of the lens. For instance, the focal length increases as an object moves closer to the lens. In addition, the thicker the lens, the more light will be bent, thereby shortening the focal length. Although the powers of the cornea and humors (aqueous and vitreous) to refract light are constant, the lens is highly elastic, so its curvature can be changed. This, in turn, alters its refractive power, allowing the eye to finely focus the image of a near or distant object.

FOCUSING FOR DISTANT VISION

Our eyes are actually best adapted for distant vision. In other words, the lens does not have to change its shape when we look at a distant object. For a normal eye, the distance beyond which no change in lens shape is necessary is about 6 meters (roughly 20 ft). This is because, beyond that point, light approaches the eyes as nearly parallel rays and can be focused on the retina by the fixed refractory structures (the cornea and humors). Thus, when we look at a distant object, the ciliary muscles of the iris will relax, which allows the elastic lens to be stretched flat, providing the least ability to refract light.

DID YOU KNOW?

Refraction of light is necessary for proper image formation; that is, refraction of light helps our eyes focus an image on the retina. As light enters the eye, it passes from a medium with an index of refraction of 1.00 (air) to a structure with a refraction index of 1.38 (the cornea). The difference between these two media makes the light rays bend significantly. The refractive index of the aqueous humor is 1.33, close to that of the cornea; therefore, it does not greatly alter the path of light after it leaves the cornea. The lens has a refractive index of 1.40, slightly higher than that of the aqueous humor. Thus, it is actually the cornea that refracts most of the light that strikes the eye. However, the lens's refractive abilities are needed for fine-tuning an image, especially as you shift your focus between distant and near objects. The importance of the cornea's ability to refract light can be observed when you open your eyes underwater. You cannot see clearly underwater because the cornea's refractive index is very close to that of water; light is essentially passing from one watery medium to another. To increase the difference between the cornea and the water and thus see more clearly, you can wear goggles or a face mask.

YOUR HEALTH: MYOPIA AND HYPEROPIA

Visual problems related to refraction can result from structural abnormalities of the eyeball (Figure 7.1). For instance, if the eyeball is too deep or if the resting curvature of the lens is too great, the image of a distant object will form in front of the retina. This will cause the individual to see distant objects as blurry, but the person's vision will be normal at close range because the lens is able to accommodate. This condition is known as **myopia**, or nearsightedness. Myopia can be treated with eyeglasses that have a diverging (concave) lens. In addition, a short laser surgery (radial keratotomy or LASIK) can be used to flatten the cornea slightly, decreasing its refractive properties.

In contrast to myopia, **hyperopia**, or farsightedness, occurs when the eyeball is too shallow or the lens too flat. In this case, parallel rays of light are focused behind the retina. People with hyperopia can see distant objects well; however, the lens cannot provide enough refraction power at close range. This is because the diverging light rays of a nearby object are focused so far behind the retina that the lens cannot bring the focal point onto the retina even at its full refractory power. Hyperopia can be corrected by eyeglasses with a converging (convex) lens.

Finally, **astigmatism** occurs when the cornea or lens fails to refract light properly, which can distort the visual image. This usually happens when the degree of curvature in the cornea or lens varies from one axis to another. For instance, the vertical axis may be more strongly curved than the horizontal axis. Fortunately, this visual problem can be corrected with eyeglasses or special contact lenses.

Figure 7.1   *(opposite page)* Light rays entering the eye are refracted (bent) by the cornea and lens so that they meet on the retina. However, in nearsightedness, or myopia, the eyeball is too long and the light rays meet in front of the retina. In contrast, in farsightedness, or hyperopia, the light rays meet behind the retina.

Hyperopic (smaller eyeball)

Point of focus

Focus falls behind
the back of the eye

"Perfect eye"

Point of focus

Focus falls on
the back of the eye

Myopic (larger eyeball)

Point of focus

Focus falls in front of
the back of the eye

FOCUSING FOR CLOSE VISION

The lens must make adjustments for close vision (less than 6 meters, or about 20 ft, away) because light rays from a close object diverge as they approach the eyes. In fact, close vision requires three adjustments to be made at the same time: (1) constriction of the pupils, which limits the divergence of light rays, forcing them to pass though the center of the lens; (2) convergence of the eyeballs; and (3) accommodation of the lens. **Accommodation** refers to the lens's ability to change its shape in order to keep the focal length constant by increasing its ability to refract light.

During accommodation, the lens gets rounder. This, in turn, increases its refractory power, enabling it to focus a nearby image on the retina. Accommodation is done through contraction of the ciliary muscles, which allows the elastic lens to become more spherical in shape. For normal vision (**emmetropia**), the lens is about 3.6 mm (0.14 in.) thick. In contrast, during accommodation, the lens thickens to about 4.5 mm (0.18 in.). One consequence of reading or other close work is that it requires almost continuous accommodation, pupillary constriction, and eye convergence. This explains why prolonged periods of reading tire the eye muscles and can result in eyestrain.

The closest point on which we can focus is thus limited by the maximum bulge the lens can achieve. This is determined by the degree of elasticity in the lens, which, unfortunately, decreases with age. Children can usually focus on something only 7 to 9 mm (0.28 to 0.25 in.) from the eye. However, as we get older, the lens tends to become stiffer and less responsive. A young adult may be able to focus on objects about 15 to 20 mm (0.59 to 0.79 in.) away, but by the time we reach the age of 50 or 60 years, the lens essentially loses the ability to accommodate, a condition known as presbyopia. In this case, the near point is typically about 80 cm (31 in.), which explains why most older people require reading glasses.

ANATOMY OF RODS AND CONES

Light focused on the retina stimulates photoreceptor cells. Rods and cones have a similar structure in that they both have an outer and an inner segment (Figure 7.2). The **outer segment** is the receptor region, essentially a highly modified cilium specialized to absorb light. This specialization includes hundreds to thousands of flattened membrane plates, or disks, which dramatically increase the membrane surface area. The names "rod" and "cone" refer to the shape of the outer segment when viewed under a microscope: In rods, the outer segment is slender and rod-shaped; in cones, it is shorter and conical. The **inner segment** of both photoreceptors is connected to the outer segment by a narrow connecting stalk. The inner segment corresponds to the cell body of a nerve cell and contains all the usual cellular organelles, including a nucleus. It also makes contact with other cells in the retina.

DID YOU KNOW?

Visual acuity is a measure of the resolving power of the eye rated against a standard of 20/20 vision. A person with 20/20 vision can see details at a distance of 20 feet. An individual is considered to have better than average vision if he or she can see that detail at a distance greater than 20 feet. For instance, 20/15 vision indicates that a person can see items at a distance of 20 feet that would be clear to a normal eye at a distance no farther than 15 feet. In contrast, a person with 20/30 vision must be 20 feet from an object to see the detail that a normal person could make out at a distance of 30 feet. A person is considered legally blind when visual acuity is worse than 20/200. Sometimes visual acuity is affected by "floaters," small spots that drift across the field of vision. They are generally temporary phenomena resulting from blood cells or cellular debris floating within the vitreous humor.

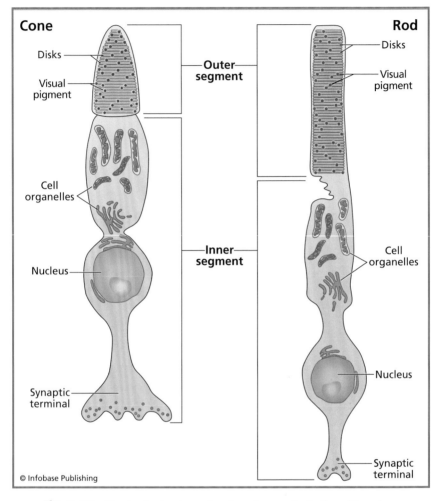

Figure 7.2 The basic structure of rods and cones is similar, although their shapes are different. They also differ in their visual pigments.

Rods and cones are "wired" to other retinal neurons differently. For instance, up to 100 rods may connect to a single ganglion cell. As a result, the output of rods is considered as a whole, which leads to vision that is fuzzy and indistinct. In contrast, each cone in the fovea has a single, straight pathway to a ganglion cell. As a result, each cone essentially has its own "labeled line" to the higher visual centers in the brain.

VISUAL PIGMENTS

The disks of the outer segment of rods and cones contain special organic compounds called **visual pigments** that change shape when they absorb light. In fact, the absorption of photons by visual pigments is the first step in the process of photoreception. The visual pigment found in rods is called **rhodopsin**, or visual purple, because it looks deep purple in color when exposed to light. Rhodopsin consists of two major parts: an **opsin** protein bound to the pigment **retinal**, which is made from vitamin A. Although rhodopsin absorbs all wavelengths of visible light, it has a peak absorption at 500 nm (green), and neural inputs from rods are only perceived as gray tones.

The visual pigments of cones all have the same retinal pigment as rods. However, the retinal is attached to different forms of opsin, and the various forms of opsin are composed of different sequences of amino acids, which determine the specific wavelengths of light that can be absorbed by the retinal pigment. Human beings have three different kinds of cones that are identical in appearance but that absorb different wavelengths of light. It is the differential stimulation of populations of cones by light that is the basis of color vision.

PHOTORECEPTION IN RODS

Retinal has two distinct three-dimensional shapes. In darkness and when bound to opsin, retinal has a bent shape and is known as *cis*-**retinal**. However, when retinal absorbs sufficient energy from a photon of light, it is converted to a straight form called the *trans*-**retinal** and is temporarily released from opsin. Amazingly, the change from *cis*- to *trans*-retinal is the only light-dependent step in photoreception and is responsible for initiating several enzymatic steps that ultimately lead to electrical events resulting in vision.

Intact rhodopsin accumulates in the dark. It is arranged in a single layer in the membranes of each disk in the outer segments of rods. When rhodopsin absorbs light, it quickly fades to a colorless compound, a process called bleaching.

Bleaching results from the conversion of retinal from its *cis* form to its *trans* form. When this occurs, the *trans*-retinal physically separates from the opsin protein and is transported to the pigment epithelium at the back of the retina. The *trans*-retinal is converted back to *cis*-retinal in an energy-requiring process, and the *cis*-retinal is then transported to the rod outer segment and reunited with an opsin molecule.

What is the significance of separating *trans*-retinal from opsin? The freed opsin (but not opsin bound to retinal) is able to activate an enzyme that in turn causes the closing of Na^+-selective ion channels, decreasing the rate of Na^+ entry into the cell and thereby hyperpolarizing the cell membrane (i.e., making the inside of the cell more negative relative to the outside). As the photoreceptor membrane hyperpolarizes, the rate at which chemical messengers (neurotransmitter molecules) are released decreases, which is the signal to bipolar cells that the photoreceptor has absorbed a photon.

For a rod to continue to function, it must regenerate rhodopsin at a rate that keeps pace with bleaching. It takes about

DID YOU KNOW?

Retinal is made from vitamin A. The pigmented layer in the sensory tunic stores vitamin A, and the body as a whole has enough vitamin A to last for several months. However, if you don't get enough vitamin A in your diet, your amount of visual pigment can decrease. Daylight vision is not typically affected because ambient light is usually bright enough to stimulate whatever visual pigments remain within the cones. On the other hand, exposure to dim light may not be enough to activate rods, causing a condition known as **night blindness**. Night blindness can dramatically impair a person's ability to drive safely in the dark. Vitamin A supplements can restore function if they are taken before the vision has actually degenerated. Carrots are a very good source of vitamin A, which explains why people may say that carrots are good for your eyes.

5 minutes to regenerate 50% of the bleached rhodopsin. Thus, bleaching contributes to the lingering visual impression after a camera's flash goes off. That is, after an intense exposure to light, a photoreceptor cannot respond to further stimulation until its rhodopsin molecules have been regenerated. Bleaching is seldom noticed under ordinary circumstances because the eyes are constantly making small involuntary changes in position that move the image across the retinal surface. In addition, because cones are less dependent on the pigment epithelium, they can regenerate half of their pigment in about 90 seconds.

COLOR VISION

Most nocturnal vertebrates (animals that are active at night) have only rods. However, many animals that are active during the day have cones and, therefore, color vision. Humans have three types of cones, each with its own visual pigment. The retinal molecule is the same for all three types of cones, but the opsins differ. The opsins determine which wavelengths (colors) of light are absorbed best. The names of the cones reflect these wavelengths. **Blue cones** respond best to wavelengths of light around 420 nm, **green cones** to wavelengths around 530 nm, and **red cones** to wavelengths around 565 nm (Figure 7.3). Note that the wavelengths of light absorbed by the three types of cones overlap, which is important for color vision. That is, we perceive hues such as orange, yellow, and purple when more than one cone is activated at the same time. For instance, yellow light causes a combination of inputs from green cones (highly stimulated), red cones (somewhat stimulated), and blue cones (relatively unaffected). An object appears to have a particular color because it reflects photons from one portion of the visible spectrum and absorbs the rest, and it is those reflected photons that stimulate cones. If photons of all colors bounce off an object and all cones are stimulated equally, we see white. In contrast, if all the photons are absorbed by an object so that none reaches the retina, the object will appear black.

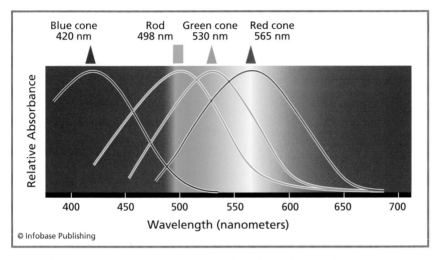

Figure 7.3   Photoreceptors contain unique visual pigments. As a result, they absorb different wavelengths of light and have different thresholds for activation. This chart shows the wavelengths to which each type of cone—blue, green, and red—responds best.

LIGHT AND DARK ADAPTATION

An important adaptation of our visual system is the ability to adjust its sensitivity to light with changes in the intensity of illumination. For instance, in low-intensity light, relatively little rhodopsin is bleached, and the retina can respond continuously to stimuli. However, if you go from a dark room into a brightly lit area, there will be a massive bleaching of visual pigments, causing the light to seem unbearably bright. At this point, rods essentially become nonfunctional. In response, pupils quickly constrict to reduce the intensity of stimulation. Soon, color vision and visual acuity develop, a phenomenon known as **light adaptation**. Within about 60 seconds, cones are sufficiently excited by bright light to take over, although they may not work at full capacity for up to 5 to 10 minutes—the time needed for pigment bleaching to adjust retinal sensitivity to this new light intensity. Therefore, during light adaptation, rod function is lost, but visual acuity is gained.

In contrast, **dark adaptation** is needed when you move from a well-lit area to a dark room. Dark adaptation is essentially the reverse of light adaptation. At first, we see nothing because our cones stop functioning in low-intensity light and our rods' pigments are still in a bleached state from the previous bright light. However, once in the dark, rhodopsin accumulates as it regenerates faster than it is bleached, and the sensitivity of rods begins to increase. Dark adaptation is slower than light adaptation and can continue for several hours, although the process is typically complete within 20 to 30 minutes, the amount of rhodopsin regenerated is sufficient to have reached almost the maximum possible sensitivity in dark. The visual system also responds by dilating pupils, which helps let more light

YOUR HEALTH: COLOR BLINDNESS

From an evolutionary perspective, color vision is advantageous under a number of conditions. For instance, color vision would potentially help diurnal (active during daylight) animals see other animals (predators or prey) trying to camouflage themselves. Color vision also would help with finding food, such as brightly colored berries contrasting against green foliage. In addition, in some animals color is important for reproduction (e.g., the colorful plumage of many male birds). However, nocturnal animals generally lack cones and thus color vision.

Although the eyes of human beings house three different types of cones, some people are unable to distinguish certain colors and are considered **color blind**. The most common cause of color blindess is the result of a recessive, sex-linked, inherited lack of one or more of the cone types. About 8 to 10% of males and about 0.5% of females have some form of color blindness. The most common type is red-green color blindness, resulting from an absence of visual pigment in either red or green cones. In this case, red and green are seen as the same color—either reddish or greenish, depending on the type of cone that is present.

into the eyes. When fully dark-adapted, the visual system is extremely sensitive. For instance, a single rod will hyperpolarize in response to a single photon of light, and as few as seven rods absorbing photons at one time will be perceived as a flash of light. In addition to the above, there are a variety of central nervous system responses to further adjust light sensitivity for different conditions. Altogether, the entire system may increase its efficiency by a factor of more than 1 million.

CONNECTIONS

Our eyes respond to the part of the electromagnetic spectrum called visible light. Light is actually composed of small packets of energy called photons. The speed of light is constant in a given medium; however, when light passes from one transparent medium into another with a different density, its speed changes. These changes of speed cause light to bend, or refract, when it meets the surface of a different medium at an oblique angle.

The lens of the eye is convex and bends incoming light rays so that they converge at a single point on the retina called the focal point. The distance between the center of the lens and its focal point is called the focal length. Although the refractory power of the cornea and humors are constant, the lens is highly elastic, allowing its curvature to change. This, in turn, alters its refractive power so that fine focusing of an image can occur.

Our eyes are actually best adapted for distant vision. For a normal eye, the distance beyond which no change in lens shape is necessary is about 6 meters (roughly 20 ft). The lens must make adjustments for close vision, which requires three simultaneous changes: constriction of the pupils, convergence of the eyeballs, and accommodation of the lens. Accommodation refers to the ability of the lens to change its shape in order to keep the focal length constant. The closest point on which we can focus clearly is called the near point of vision. It is limited by the maximum bulge that the lens can achieve, and is determined by the degree of elasticity in the lens. By the age of 50 or 60, the lens no longer accommodates, a condition known as presbyopia.

Light focused on the retina stimulates photoreceptor cells. Both rods and cones have an outer segment and an inner segment. The outer segment is the receptor region and contains flattened membrane disks, which have visual pigment molecules that can change their shape when they absorb light. The inner segment of both photoreceptors makes contact with other cells in the retina. The disks of the outer segment of rods and cones contain special organic compounds called visual pigments. The absorption of photons by visual pigments is the first step in the process of photoreception. Visual pigments are derived from the compound rhodopsin, which consists of an opsin protein bound to the pigment retinal. Cones have the same retinal pigment as rods, but different forms of opsin. Retinal can assume two distinct three-dimensional shapes. In darkness and when bound to opsin, retinal has a bent shape and is called *cis*-retinal. However, when retinal absorbs the energy of a photon of light, it is converted to a straight form called *trans*-retinal. This process, called bleaching, involves the separated *trans*-retinal being transported to the pigment epithelium at the rear of the retina. It is then converted again to *cis*-retinal, in an energy-requiring process, transported back to the rod outer segment, and reunited with opsin.

After bleaching, the freed opsin activates enzymes that help hyperpolarize the cell membrane. As the membrane hyperpolarizes, the rate of neurotransmitter release decreases, telling bipolar cells that the photoreceptor has absorbed a photon.

Humans have three types of cone cells—blue, green, and red—and the name of each cone reflects the wavelengths of light it absorbs best. The wavelengths of light absorbed by the three cones overlap, and perception of hues results when more than one cone is activated at the same time.

The sensitivity of our visual system varies with the intensity of illumination. Light adaptation occurs when you go from a dark room into bright light; dark adaptation is needed when you move from a well-lit area to a dark room.

8

Sense of Hearing

THE SENSE OF HEARING ALLOWS US TO DETECT AND INTERPRET sound waves, which result from vibrating air molecules. This sense is necessary in normal human life because hearing and speech are important means of communication and the basis of complex social interactions. In fact, a loss of hearing can result in unfortunate behavioral disturbances.

PROPERTIES OF SOUND

Sound, defined as any audible vibration of molecules, is essentially made up of pressure disturbances in the form of alternating areas of high and low pressure. Because sound, unlike light, depends on vibrating molecules, it cannot pass through a vacuum, but it can be transmitted though water, solids, and air. Sound also travels much more slowly than light does—about 331 m/s (0.2 miles/s) in dry air, compared to 300,000 km/s (about 186,000 miles/s) for light. For this reason, a lightning flash is seen almost instantly after it occurs, but the sound it creates (thunder) reaches our ears more slowly. In fact, each second that passes between a lightning bolt and its thunderclap indicates that a storm is about one-fifth of a mile farther away.

Sound is transmitted by a vibrating object, such as a tuning fork, loudspeaker, or vocal cords. For instance, if you strike a tuning fork, its prongs move back and forth. As the prongs move forward, they push air molecules closer together, producing a high-density area called a zone of compression. In contrast, as the prongs rebound, they create a less dense region called a zone of rarefaction. Thus, a vibrating object produces a series of compressions and rarefactions, collectively called a **sound wave**, which moves outward in all directions. Individual molecules do not travel from the vibrating object to our eardrum. Instead, a molecule collides with its neighbor, and they create a ripple-like effect, similar to the surface of water when you throw a stone into it. The sensations we perceive as pitch and loudness of sound are related to the physical properties—the frequency and amplitude—of these vibrations.

PITCH

Frequency, expressed in **hertz** (**Hz**), or cycles per second, is defined as the number of waves that pass a given point over a period of time (Figure 8.1). The distance between two consecutive wave crests (or troughs) is called the **wavelength** of sound, and it is constant for a particular tone. For instance, the frequency of middle C on a piano is 261 Hz. Frequency and wavelength have inverse relationships. This means that the shorter the wavelength, the higher the frequency of a sound.

The human ear can hear frequencies between 20 and 20,000 Hz, and our ears are most sensitive to frequencies between 500 and 4,000 Hz (in that range, we can distinguish frequencies that differ by only 2 to 3 Hz). **Pitch** is our sense of whether a sound is high or low, and is determined by the frequency of sound waves. That is, the higher the frequency, the higher the pitch. Most sounds we hear are mixtures of several frequencies.

LOUDNESS

Loudness is the perception of sound energy—that is, the pressure difference between the compressed and rarefied areas.

It is indicated by the **amplitude**, or the height of sound waves (refer again to Figure 8.1). Loudness is expressed in units called **decibels (dB)**. By convention, 0 dB is arbitrarily set to be the threshold of human hearing. Every 10 dB step increase represents a sound that is 10 times more intense. For instance,

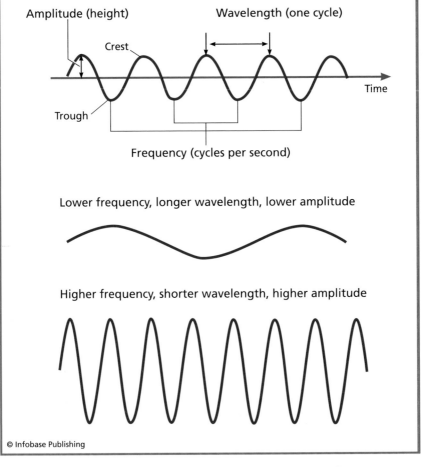

Figure 8.1 A pure tone has periodic crests and troughs. The distance between two consecutive crests is called the wavelength, and it is constant for a specific tone. Frequency, expressed in hertz (Hz), is the number of waves that pass a certain point within a given time period (usually 1 second). The range of frequencies most humans can hear is from 20 to 20,000 Hz.

30 dB is 10 times louder than 20 dB and 100 times louder than 10 dB. Normal conversation is about 60 dB, and the threshold for pain caused by sound is around 130 dB. Prolonged exposure to sounds greater than 90 dB can lead to permanent loss of hearing.

THE OUTER EAR

The ear is divided into three major regions: the outer ear, middle ear, and inner ear (Figure 8.2). The first two structures are concerned only with the transmission of sound to the inner ear, which houses the receptors that actually turn fluid motion into action potentials (nerve impulses).

The **outer ear** is essentially a funnel for conducting air vibrations to the eardrum. It consists of the auricle, lobule, external auditory canal, and tympanic membrane. The **auricle**, or pinna, is the part that most people think of as the ear. It is composed of elastic cartilage covered with skin. The fleshy **lobule** (earlobe) lacks cartilage.

The **external auditory canal**, or ear canal, is a curved tube about 2.5 to 3 cm (about 1.0 to 1.2 in.) long in adults. Although it is supported by cartilage at its opening, the remainder consists of a canal carved in the temporal bone of the skull. The canal is lined with skin bearing hair, sebaceous glands, and modified sweat glands called **ceruminous glands**. The secretions from these glands form a sticky, bitter substance called **cerumen**, or earwax, which traps foreign particles, repels insects, and slows the growth of microorganisms, thereby reducing the chance of infection. Normally, cerumen dries and falls from the canal. However, it sometimes becomes impacted and interferes with hearing.

Sound waves entering the canal eventually reach the **tympanic membrane**, or eardrum, which is a boundary between the outer and middle ear. This membrane is about 1 cm (0.4 in.) in diameter and is slightly concave on its outer surface, giving it a conical appearance. Sound waves make the eardrum vibrate, and the greater the intensity of sound, the further the membrane is displaced.

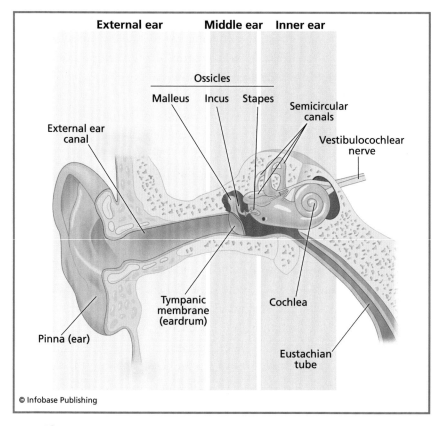

External ear   **Middle ear**   **Inner ear**

Ossicles

Malleus   Incus   Stapes

External ear
canal

Semicircular
canals

Vestibulocochlear
nerve

Tympanic
membrane
(eardrum)

Cochlea

Pinna (ear)

Eustachian
tube

© Infobase Publishing

Figure 8.2   The outer ear funnels sound waves into the external ear canal. The three tiny bones of the middle ear, the ossicles, act as a lever system, raising the pressure exerted on the oval window—the place where the inner ear begins. The inner ear contains the cochlea, a structure that turns pressure waves into electrical signals that allow us to perceive sound.

THE MIDDLE EAR

The **middle ear,** a small, air-filled space, is located in the **tympanic cavity** of the temporal bone. The anterior wall of the middle ear contains the opening of the **auditory tube,** or Eustachian tube, a passageway to the area of the upper throat behind the ear. Normally, this tube is flattened and closed.

However, swallowing and yawning open it briefly and allow air to enter or leave the tympanic cavity, which makes the pressure on both sides of the eardrum equal. This is important because the eardrum does not vibrate freely unless the pressure of both of its surfaces is the same. You may notice the "ear-popping" sensation of pressure equalizing when you change altitude (e.g., driving up a mountain road or flying on an airplane).

The middle ear also contains the three smallest bones in the human body, which span the 2- to 3-mm distance from the eardrum to the inner ear. The bones are called **ossicles**, and they are named for their shapes. The **malleus** (the hammer) is attached to the inner surface of the eardrum and joins with the **incus** (the anvil), which, in turn, joins with the **stapes** (the stirrup). The base of the stapes fits into the **oval window**, where the inner ear begins. The function of the ossicles is to transmit the vibrating motion of the eardrum to the oval window. Because the tympanic membrane is about 20 times larger in diameter than the oval window, a movement in the tympanic membrane produces a 20-times-larger deflection at the base of the stapes.

Two tiny skeletal muscles associated with the ossicles are also found in the middle ear. The **tensor tympani** comes out of the wall of the auditory tube and attaches to the malleus, while the **stapedius** originates from the rear wall of the cavity and joins with the stapes. When the ears are exposed to very loud sounds, these muscles contract reflexively to prevent damage to the hearing receptors in the inner ear. In particular, the tensor tympani tenses the eardrum and the stapedius limits the vibration of the whole ossicle chain, thereby limiting the movement of the stapes on the oval window. This reflex probably evolved, in part, for protection from loud but slowly developing noises, such as thunder, because it has a latency period of about 40 milliseconds (msec), which is not quick enough to protect the inner ear from sudden noises such as gunshots.

THE INNER EAR

The **inner ear** is housed deep within the temporal bone and contains receptors for the senses of hearing and equilibrium (equilibrium will be discussed in Chapter 9). The inner ear has two major divisions: the bony labyrinth and the membranous labyrinth. The **bony labyrinth** is a maze of passageways in the temporal bone and includes the cochlea, the vestibule, and the semicircular canals. Only the cochlea will be discussed here; the other two structures have to do with the sense of equilibrium.

The **membranous labyrinth** is a continuous series of fluid-filled membranous sacs and ducts inside the bony labyrinth. The fluid in the membranous labyrinth, called **endolymph**, contains different electrolytes than most other body fluids. It is high in potassium and low in sodium. Between the bony and membranous labyrinths is a cushion of fluid called the **perilymph**. Together, endolymph and perilymph are responsible for conducting the sound vibrations involved in hearing.

YOUR HEALTH: MIDDLE EAR PROBLEMS

A middle ear inflammation (**otitis media**) is a fairly common result of a sore throat, especially in children, whose auditory tubes are shorter and run more horizontally than those of adults. In fact, otitis media is the most common cause of hearing loss in children; cases are often treated with antibiotics. However, ear tubes (small, hollow, spool-shaped plastic structures) may be suggested for children who have chronic ear infections. A specialist (otolaryngologist) places the tubes through a small surgical opening made in the eardrum while the child is under general anesthesia.

Tinnitus is the sensation of a ringing or clicking sound in the ears when no outside sound really exists. It can be a symptom of nerve denegation, the result of otitis media, or a side effect of some medications, such as aspirin.

The **cochlea** (Latin for "snail") is a spiral, cone-shaped, bony chamber about half the size of a garden pea (Figure 8.3a). Its outer shell makes 2.5 turns around a central bony pillar, giving it a snail-like appearance. The cochlea has three fluid-filled chambers, called scala, separated by membranes (Figure 8.3b). Running through the center of the cochlea is a wormlike chamber called the **scala media**, which ends blindly at the cochlear apex. The scala media houses the **organ of Corti** (Figure 8.3c), which is the actual receptor organ for the sense of hearing. The upper chamber in the cochlea is called the **scala vestibuli**, and it connects with the oval window. Finally, the lower chamber, the **scala tympani**, ends at the **round window**, a membrane that separates the inner ear from the middle ear. Because the scala media is part of the membranous labyrinth, it is filled with endolymph. However, the scala vestibuli and scala tympani are part of the bony labyrinth and thus contain perilymph. These two chambers communicate with each other through a narrow channel at the cochlear apex.

The scala media is separated from the scala vestibuli above by a thin **vestibular membrane.** It is separated from the scala tympani below by a much thicker **basilar membrane**, which supports the organ of Corti. The basilar membrane is narrow and thick near the oval window and gradually becomes wider and thinner as it approaches the cochlear apex. This structural change is important for sound reception.

The organ of Corti converts sound vibrations into nerve impulses. It has an epithelium made of four rows of **hair cells** and supporting cells. Hair cells get their name from their **stereocilia**, the long, stiff microvilli at their top. Hair cells are not neurons, but rather they do synapse with nerve fibers at their base. The hair cells are arranged by function, with about 3,500 **inner hair cells** forming a single row. Each of these hair cells has a cluster of 50 to 60 stereocilia, arranged from short to tall. Approximately 12,000–20,000 **outer hair cells** form three rows across from the inner hair cells. Each outer hair cell has about 100 stereocilia grouped in the shape of the letter

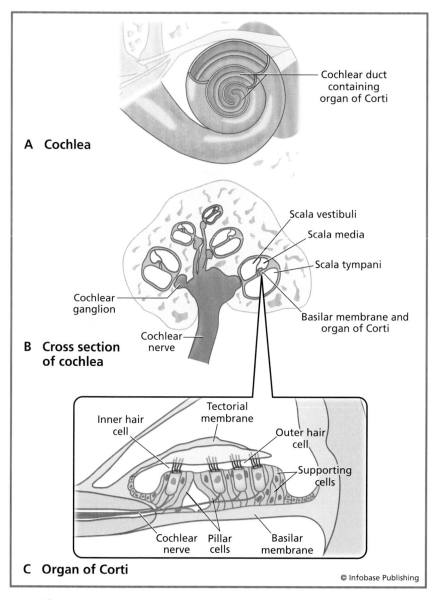

A Cochlea

Cochlear duct containing organ of Corti

Scala vestibuli

Scala media

Scala tympani

Cochlear ganglion

Basilar membrane and organ of Corti

Cochlear nerve

B Cross section of cochlea

Tectorial membrane

Inner hair cell

Outer hair cell

Supporting cells

Cochlear nerve

Pillar cells

Basilar membrane

C Organ of Corti

© Infobase Publishing

Figure 8.3 The organ of Corti (c), which is housed inside the cochlea (a and b), is the receptor organ for hearing. It is made up of supporting cells and about 20,000 hearing receptor cells called hair cells, all of which play specialized roles in the sense of hearing.

"V." Resting on top of the stereocilia is a gelatinous **tectorial membrane**, and the entire structure sits on top of the basilar membrane. The stereocilia thus protrude into the potassium (K^+)-rich endolymph, and the longest of them are embedded in the overlying tectorial membrane. It turns out that what we hear only comes from the inner hair cells that send their signals by means of sensory nerve fibers of the cochlear nerve, which runs from the organ of Corti to the brain. The outer hair cells adjust the response of the cochlea to different frequencies, allowing the inner hair cells to work with greater precision.

TRANSMISSION OF SOUND TO THE INNER EAR

Before describing the physiology of hearing, which involves exciting the hair cells in the organ of Corti, it is necessary to discuss how sound is transmitted. Airborne sound waves enter the external auditory canal and strike the tympanic membrane. This causes the membrane to vibrate at the same frequency as the sound wave; the amplitude of the vibration depends on how intense the sound is. The motion of the eardrum is then transmitted to the oval window through the ossicles of the middle ear.

We might ask why sound waves don't hit the oval window directly—that is, why do we need ossicles? The answer has to do with the fluid-filled chambers behind the oval window. The eardrum vibrates easily because it is surrounded by air. In contrast, the oval window has to vibrate against the fluid (perilymph) of the inner ear. Because this fluid puts up a much greater resistance to motion than air does, if sound waves struck the oval window directly, there would not be enough energy to overcome the resistance.

The ossicles, which act as a system of pistons, transfer the same total force that hits the tympanic membrane to the oval window. However, because the tympanic membrane is about 20 times larger than the oval window, the pressure per unit area exerted on the oval window is about 20 times that on the eardrum. This increased pressure overcomes the resistance of the cochlear fluid, making it vibrate. As mentioned earlier, the ossicles also help protect the ear from the effects of a loud noise (through the action of two tiny skeletal muscles). The middle ear muscles also help coordinate speech with hearing. Without them, the sound of our own speech would be so loud that it could damage the inner ear. To prevent this, just as we are about to speak, the brain signals these muscles to contract.

As the stapes rocks back and forth against the oval window, it sets the perilymph in the scala vestibuli into a similar motion. In this way, pressure waves travel through the perilymph from the basal end toward the narrow channel at the cochlear apex. Sounds of very low frequency (below 20 Hz) create pressure waves that go all the way through the perilymph of the cochlea to the round window. Such sounds do not activate the organ of Corti because they are below the threshold of hearing. However, sounds of higher frequency create pressure waves that go through the scala media into the perilymph of the scala tympani. As these pressure waves move through the scala media, they make the basilar membrane vibrate, thereby exciting the organ of Corti. Each time this occurs, the pressure waves make the round window bulge into the middle ear cavity, which acts like a pressure valve, dissipating the fluid vibration. This prevents us from hearing an echoing sound every time we hear something.

PHYSIOLOGY OF HEARING

To produce a sensation of sound, the hair cells of the organ of Corti must be excited. This happens when pressure waves are transmitted through the scala media, which causes the basilar membrane to vibrate. Keep in mind that the tips of the longest stereocilia of hair cells are embedded in the tectorial membrane, which is anchored in place. As a result, the tectorial membrane remains relatively still as the basilar membrane and hair cells vibrate up and down. Consequently, as it moves, the basilar membrane bends the stereocilia back and forth, pressing them against the tectorial membrane.

Sound stimuli turn into voltage changes when the stereocilia are deflected by movements of the basilar membrane. This is possible because the tips of stereocilia of inner hair cells contain integral membrane proteins that function as mechanically gated ion channels (passageways that open when the stereocilia bend). In addition, a fine protein filament called a *tip link* extends like a spring from an ion channel of a stereocilium to one next to it. So, when a taller stereocilium bends away from a short one, it pulls on the tip link, thus opening the ion channel of the shorter stereocilium.

YOUR HEALTH: DEAFNESS

Any hearing loss is considered **deafness**. However, there are two main types of deafness—conduction deafness and sensorineural deafness—which differ in their causes. **Conduction deafness** occurs when sound transmission (conductance) has trouble reaching the fluids of the inner ear. This can result from a buildup of earwax or a ruptured eardrum. However, the two most common causes are middle ear inflammations (infections) and **otosclerosis** of the ossicles. Otosclerosis happens when too much bony tissue grows and fuses the stapes to the oval window or fuses the ossicles to one another. Conduction deafness can usually be treated with a hearing aid or surgery.

Sensorineural deafness happens when neural structures, including hair cells, cochlear nerve fibers, and auditory brain cells, get damaged. For instance, being exposed for a long time to high-intensity sound, such as jet engines, makes the stereocilia stiffen and tear. Sensorineural deafness also can happen when the cochlear nerve degenerates, or if a person suffers a stroke or a brain tumor. Some of these conditions may be treated with a cochlear implant, which converts sound energy to electrical signals, bypassing the organ of Corti, and sends them directly to the appropriate region of the brain.

The most common ion in endolymph is K^+. Consequently, when these channels are opened, they cause an inward flow of K^+, bringing in positive charge and thereby depolarizing the hair cell. In contrast, when the stereocilium bends the other way, its channel closes, and the cell repolarizes. Depolarization makes a hair cell release more neurotransmitter, which stimulates the sensory dendrites at its base. This, in turn, causes the cochlear fibers to send a faster stream of impulses to the brain, which are interpreted as sound.

As mentioned above, the basilar membrane is not uniform in shape. It is narrower and thicker near the oval window. It also has collagen fibers that span its width, similar to the strings of a piano or harp. This arrangement gives the entire structure different resonant properties along its length. As a result, the membrane is displaced most at the point where its fibers are most "tuned" to a particular sound frequency. For instance, fibers near the oval window are short and stiff, so they resonate in response to high-frequency pressure waves. On the other hand, the longer, floppier basilar membrane fibers near the cochlear apex resonate in time with lower-frequency pressure waves. In this way, the basilar membrane mechanically processes sound signals before they reach the receptors, the hair cells of the organ of Corti. In other words, signals sent from hair cells near the oval window are perceived as having a high pitch, whereas signals originating from hair cells near the cochlear apex are heard as low pitch sound.

SENSORY CODING

We are able to distinguish pitch and loudness and to figure out where a sound is coming from. The perception of pitch results from the properties of the resonance basilar membrane, which allows the hair cells in different parts of the organ of Corti to be activated by sound waves of different frequencies. Impulses from specific hair cells are then interpreted as particular pitches by the auditory cortex in the brain. When a sound is made up of tones of many frequencies, several groups of hair cells are activated at the same time.

Our perception of loudness is a result of louder sounds producing more vigorous vibrations of the organ of Corti. This, in turn, excites a larger number of hair cells over a broader area of the basilar membrane, triggering a higher frequency of action potentials in the cochlear nerve fibers. Determining the source of sound depends on the relative intensity and timing of the sound waves reaching the two ears.

CONNECTIONS

Sound, defined as any audible vibration of molecules, is essentially made up of pressure disturbances that have alternating areas of high and low pressure. Sound can be transmitted though water, solids, and air, and travels much more slowly than light. A vibrating object produces a series of compressions and rarefactions, collectively called a sound wave, which move outward in all directions. The sensations we perceive as pitch and loudness of sound are related to the physical properties of these vibrations.

Sound can be described in terms of two physical properties: frequency and amplitude. Frequency, expressed in hertz (cycles per second), is the number of waves that pass a given point over a period of time. The distance between two consecutive wave crests (or troughs) is called the wavelength of sound, and it is constant for a particular tone. Pitch is our sense of whether a sound is high or low and is determined by the frequency of sound waves. Loudness is the perception of sound energy and is indicated by the amplitude, or height, of sound waves. Loudness is expressed in units called decibels (dB).

The ear has three major regions: the outer ear, middle ear, and inner ear. The outer ear funnels air vibrations to the eardrum. The auricle is what most people think of as

(continues)

(continued)

the ear—the outer structure composed of cartilage covered by skin, along with the fleshy earlobe called the lobule. The tympanic membrane (eardrum) forms a boundary between the outer and middle ear.

The middle ear is located in the tympanic cavity of the temporal bone. The middle ear also contains ossicles: the malleus (hammer), incus (anvil), and stapes (stirrup). The base of the stapes fits into the oval window, where the inner ear begins. The function of the ossicles is to transmit the vibratory motion of the eardrum to the oval window. Two tiny skeletal muscles associated with the ossicles—the tensor tympani and the stapedius—contract reflexively when exposed to loud sounds to prevent damage to the hearing receptors in the inner ear.

The inner ear is housed deep within the temporal bone and contains receptors for the senses of hearing and equilibrium. It includes the bony labyrinth and the membranous labyrinth. The bony labyrinth has three regions: the vestibule, the cochlea, and the semicircular canal. The membranous labyrinth is a continuous series of fluid-filled membranous sacs and ducts held within the bony labyrinth. The fluid inside the membranous labyrinth is called endolymph. Between the bony and membranous labyrinths is a cushion of fluid called the perilymph.

The cochlea is a spiral, conical, bony chamber with three fluid-filled chambers, called scala, separated by membranes. Running through the center of the cochlea is a wormlike chamber called the scala media of the membranous labyrinth, which ends blindly at the cochlear apex. The scala media houses the organ of Corti, which is the actual receptor organ for the sense of hearing. The sensation of sound is produced by the stimulation of the hair cells of the organ of Corti. The perception of pitch results from the properties of the basilar membrane, which allows for the activation of hair cells in different parts of the organ of Corti by sound waves of different frequencies.

9

Sense of Equilibrium

THE SENSE OF **equilibrium**, WHICH ALSO INVOLVES BALANCE and coordination, lets us detect the position of the head by monitoring gravity, linear acceleration, and rotation. Like the sense of hearing, equilibrium depends on mechanoreceptors (hair cells) located in the inner ear. In fact, the original function of the ear in vertebrates was for equilibrium, not hearing. During the course of evolution, the cochlea formed, along with the middle ear structures, which allowed the ear to sense sound as well as maintain balance. The sense of equilibrium also depends on the sense of vision, as well as information from stretch receptors (proprioceptors) located in skeletal muscles and tendons.

STRUCTURE FOR SENSING EQUILIBRIUM

The receptors for sensing equilibrium are found in the **vestibular apparatus** of the inner ear (Figure 9.1). This structure consists of three semicircular ducts and two chambers: the anterior saccule and the posterior utricle. The **semicircular ducts** provide sensory information about rotational movements of the head, or **dynamic equilibrium**. For instance, turning your head to the right stimulates receptors in the semicircular

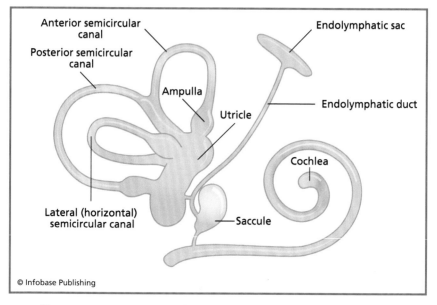

Figure 9.1   The vestibular apparatus is part of the inner ear that functions in equilibrium (balance). The three semicircular canals react when the head turns. The utricle and saccule sense movement of the head because they are sensitive to changes in gravity. These equilibrium receptors give the brain information that it can use to determine the position and movement of the head and body.

canals that provide information about how fast the movement is and in which direction. The **saccule** and **utricle** send signals to the brain about the position of the head in space with respect to gravity, which is referred to as **static equilibrium**. For example, if you tilt your head to one side, these receptors will provide information on the angle involved and whether your head is tilting forward, backward, or to one side. These receptors also are stimulated by sudden acceleration, such as when a car makes a "jack-rabbit" start. This lets us know when we are moving faster physically.

THE SACCULE AND UTRICLE
The utricle and saccule are important for monitoring the position of the head in space, and help us sense whether the

body is moving. The sensory receptors for static equilibrium are located in structures called **maculae** (singular, *macula*), which are found in the saccule and utricle. The **macula sacculi** lie nearly vertically in the wall of the saccule, and the **macula utriculi** lie almost horizontally on the floor of the utricle. These receptors are sensitive to changes in the body's rate of motion and whether the body is moving backward or forward. They do not sense rotation, however.

Each macula is a flat epithelial patch measuring about 2 by 3 mm (0.08 by 0.12 in.) that contains scattered receptor cells (hair cells) and supporting cells. Each hair cell has 40 to 70 stereocilia and one true cilium, called the **kinocilium**. The tips of the stereocilia and kinocilium are embedded in a jelly-like **otolithic membrane**. This membrane contains tiny calcium carbonate crystals called **otoliths** (literally, "ear stones"). These make the membrane denser and keep it still, which makes the receptors more sensitive to changes in gravity and motion.

ACTIVATION OF MACULAE RECEPTORS

When your head is in the normal, upright position, otoliths sit on top of the macula utriculi and stimulation is minimal. However, when you tilt your head to one side, the weight of the otolithic membrane bends the stereocilia, thereby stimulating hair cells. Any changes in orientation of the head cause a combination of stimulation of the utricles and saccules of the two ears. The brain figures out where the head is by comparing these inputs to each other and to other inputs from the eyes and proprioceptors. For instance, when you start to run, the otolithic membranes of the utricle maculae lag behind, bending the stereocilia backward. In contrast, when you stop moving, the otolithic membranes slide forward, bending the hairs in that direction. Similarly, when you are in an elevator that moves up, the otolithic membranes of the saccule briefly lag behind and pull down on the stereocilia. When the elevator stops, the membranes keep moving for an instant, bending the hairs upward. Thus, inertia of the membranes is especially important in detecting linear acceleration or deceleration; the utricle senses horizontal movement, whereas the saccule responds to vertical acceleration.

When stereocilia bend toward a kinocilium, the hair cell depolarizes and, in turn, releases more neurotransmitters. As a result, a larger number of signals are sent to the brain. In contrast, when stereocilia bend away from a kinocilium, the receptor hyperpolarizes and releases fewer neurotransmitters. It is important to note that the maculae respond only to changes in acceleration or velocity of the head. In other words, these receptors adapt quickly, so they do not provide input when the position of the head does not change.

THE SEMICIRCULAR DUCTS

Rotational acceleration is detected by the three semicircular ducts, each of which is housed in a bony **semicircular canal** of the temporal bone. The anterior and posterior semicircular ducts are positioned vertically, at right angles to each other. The lateral duct is about 30° from the horizontal plane. The location of the three canals allows a different duct to be stimulated by rotation of the head in different planes (e.g., when

YOUR HEALTH: INNER EAR INFECTION

Labyrinthitis refers to an infection or inflammation of the ear's labyrinth, the part of the inner ear that contains the fluid-filled chambers: the cochlea and the vestibular apparatus. It results in dizziness or vertigo, which has symptoms of an inability to maintain proper balance, nausea, vomiting, and temporary loss of hearing in the affected ear. Bacterial labyrinthitis may also spread to the middle ear, causing otitis media or even bacterial meningitis, and antibiotics are usually prescribed. Viral labyrinthitis tends to be self-limiting, usually disappearing within several weeks. Because there are several different underlying causes to dizziness, an examination by a physician is necessary for proper diagnosis of an inner ear infection.

you turn your head from side to side to say "no," nod it up and down to indicate "yes," or tilt it from shoulder to shoulder).

Each semicircular duct opens into the utricle. It has a swollen sac at one end called the **ampulla**, which is an expanded region that contains sensory cells. Within each ampulla is a mound of hair cells and supporting cells known as the **crista ampullaris,** or simply *crista*. The stereocilia and kinocilium are embedded in a gelatinous region called the **cupula**, which extends from a crista to the roof of the ampulla. Like the maculae, the cristae are stimulated by head movements, but in this case, rotational movements stimulate them most.

ACTIVATION OF CRISTAE RECEPTORS

The cristae respond to changes in the velocity of rotational movements of the head. When the head turns, the semicircular ducts, which contain endolymph, rotate as well. However, the endolymph lags behind for an instant, thereby pushing the cupula and bending the stereocilia. This, in turn, stimu-

YOUR HEALTH: MOTION SICKNESS

Motion sickness is a common equilibrium disorder; it can be caused by riding in a car, train, airplane, or boat. It appears to involve sensory input mismatch to the brain from the inner ears (semcircular canals), eyes, and muscle/joint proprioceptors. For instance, while reading a book in a moving car, your inner ear detects that you are moving forward, while your eyes and your proprioceptors tell your brain that you are sitting still. These conflicting signals may lead to motion sickness, causing dizziness, nausea, excessive salivation, pallor, headache, rapid breathing, and profuse sweating. Similarly, seasickness may occur because visual inputs indicate that your body is fixed with reference to your cabin, but the vestibular apparatus detects movement—hence sensory input mismatch. Over-the-counter drugs for motion sickness work by depressing input from the inner ear.

lates the hair cells to change their membrane potential (voltage). As with maculae receptors, bending stereocilia toward the kinocilium leads to a depolarization, whereas movement in the other direction causes a hyperpolarization of hair cells. Because the axes of the hair cells in complementary ducts are opposite, rotation in a particular direction causes the receptors in one ampulla of the pair to depolarize and the receptors in the other to hyperpolarize. However, after about 25 to 30 seconds of continuous rotation, the endolymph catches up with the movement of the ducts and stimulation of hair cells ceases. This explains why, when we are blindfolded, we often cannot tell whether we are moving at a constant speed or not moving at all after the first few seconds of rotation.

CONNECTIONS

The sense of equilibrium allows you to detect the position of your head in space by monitoring gravity, linear acceleration, and rotation. The receptors for equilibrium are found in the vestibular apparatus of the inner ear, which consists of three semicircular canals and two chambers called the saccule and the utricle. The semicircular canals provide information about rotational movements of the head, which is referred to as dynamic equilibrium. The saccule and utricle give the brain information about your position in space with respect to gravity, called static equilibrium. The sensory receptors for static equilibrium are patches of hair cells, called the macula sacculi and the macula utriculi, that respond to linear acceleration forces but not to rotation.

Each macula is a flat epithelial patch that contains supporting cells and scattered receptor cells (hair cells). Each hair cell has stereocilia and a true cilium called the kinocilium. The tips of the stereocilia and kinocilium are embedded in a gelatinous otolithic membrane, which is studded with tiny calcium carbonate crystals called otoliths. When the head tilts, the weight of the otolithic membrane bends the stereocilia, thereby stimulating the hair cells. The brain interprets head orientation by comparing vestibular inputs to each other and to other inputs from the eyes and stretch receptors.

Rotational acceleration is detected by the three semicircular ducts, each housed in a semicircular canal of the temporal bone. The anterior and posterior semicircular ducts are positioned at right angles to each other; the lateral duct is about 30° from the horizontal plane. The semicircular ducts are filled with endolymph and contain a swollen sac at one end called the ampulla. Within each ampulla is a mound of hair cells and supporting cells known as the crista ampullaris. The stereocilia and kinocilium are embedded in a gelatinous region called the cupula, which extends from a crista to the roof of the ampulla. The cristae respond to changes in the velocity of angular or rotational movements of the head. However, the endolymph lags behind for an instant, thereby pushing the cupula and bending the stereocilia. This, in turn, stimulates the hair cells. After about 25 to 30 seconds of continuous rotation, the endolymph catches up with the movement of the ducts and stimulation of the hair cells stops.

10

Sense of Thirst and Hunger

THE FEELINGS OF THIRST AND HUNGER ARE NOT CONNECTED to a particular sense organ like the senses of vision or hearing are. Instead, they are triggered by one or more stimuli that come from inside the body itself. For these reasons, they are often referred to as part of the general sensations. Stimuli that are strong enough to elicit general sensations also cause physiological and behavioral changes that try to reduce the intensity of such sensations. That is, stimuli for general sensations induce **drives**—motivational states that influence us to try to get whatever the body feels we lack. For instance, a lack of water in the body not only leads to a sensation of **thirst**, the desire for fluid, especially water, but it also encourages us to search for something to drink. Thus, drives associated with general sensations help us survive.

WATER BALANCE

The human adult body is roughly 70% water by weight, without taking fat deposits into account. Amazingly, healthy people have an incredible ability to maintain the concentration of their body fluids within very narrow limits. In fact, body water normally increases or decreases only about 0.22%

of the body weight. For example, in a 70-kg (154-lb) man, a typical variation of body water is only around 150 milliliters out of about 40 liters (42.3 quarts) of total body water.

In order for the body to remain properly hydrated, water intake must equal water output. Water output occurs by several routes, most of which are obligatory, meaning they cannot be prevented (Figure 10.1). For instance, some water loss occurs as water leaves directly through the skin. Obligatory water also leaves the body in the form of vapor every time we exhale. Water output through the skin and from breathing is often called **insensible water loss** because we do not consciously notice it. Additional obligatory water loss occurs when we perspire, urinate, and defecate.

The amount of water intake varies quite a bit from person to person and is influenced by personal habit as well as thirst. However, it is typically around 2.5 L (2.6 qt) per day in adults. Most of this water enters the body through liquids we drink. We also obtain water from solid foods (there is a lot of water in many fruits and vegetables), and some water is actually produced in our bodies through cellular metabolism; this is called **metabolic water**.

DID YOU KNOW?

The amount of total body water depends not only on body weight, but also on one's sex, age, and amount of body fat. For instance, infants have a relatively low amount of body fat and bone mass and, therefore, contain a greater percentage body water (about 70-75% of body weight). Total body water decreases with age, and may drop to about 45% of body weight in old age. In addition, a healthy young man is about 60% water, whereas a healthy young woman will be closer to 50%. This difference results from the relatively larger amount of body fat and smaller number of skeletal muscles in females (adipose tissue is only about 20% water, whereas skeletal muscle is roughly 65% water).

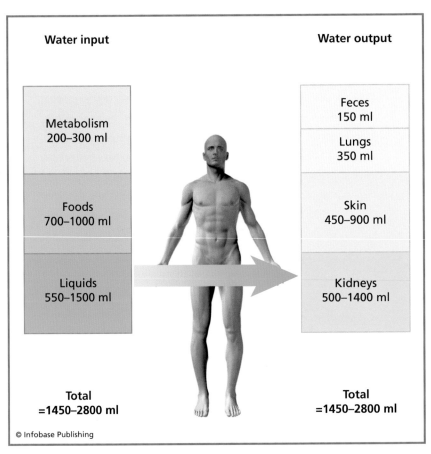

Figure 10.1   The body has a thirst mechanism to balance water intake and output. The body loses water through the processes of urination, defecation, and sweating, as well as through the skin and lungs. The amount of water we take in must equal the amount we lose. The body is amazingly efficient at balancing the water content.

REGULATION OF WATER INTAKE

Fluid intake is governed by the sensation of thirst. Unfortunately, the regulation of this sense is poorly understood. Evidence indicates that dehydration causes blood volume and pressure to drop, while blood osmolality (the concentration of dissolved solutes) rises. Some of these physical changes are detected by the **thirst center** of the hypothalamus, which contains **osmoreceptors**. Typically, when someone loses more water than 0.5% of the body weight (about 350 ml for a 70-kg person), has a 10% reduction in plasma volume, or has an increase of 1–2% in plasma osmolality, it will be enough to cause a dry mouth and stimulate the thirst center. A dry mouth occurs as a direct result of an increase in plasma osmolality because this condition inhibits fluid flow from blood vessels. Because the salivary glands obtain water from the blood, less saliva is produced when we are dehydrated. However, it is not certain whether our primary motivation to drink is simply a dry mouth. For instance, studies show that people who do not secrete saliva and experimental animals that have had their salivary ducts tied off do not drink any more than normal individuals do (except when they eat because they need water to moisten food).

The hypothalamic thirst center is stimulated when its osmoreceptor cells lose water to the extracellular fluid. This loss of water causes the cells to depolarize, presumably leading to a sensation of thirst, thereby motivating us to drink. The thirst center also responds to angiotensin II, a hormone that has several complementary actions that work to stabilize blood pressure and extracellular fluid volume. This is accomplished, in part, by baroreceptors and osmoreceptors in the **juxtaglomerular apparatus** of the kidneys; these structures release the enzyme **renin** into the bloodstream in response to a drop in blood pressure (volume) or to a decrease in plasma osmolality. Renin converts a circulating plasma protein, angiotensinogen, into angiotensin I, which is then converted into the active form, angiotensin II, as the molecule passes through the pulmonary circuit to and from the lungs. In addition to stimulating the thirst center, angiotensin II is a potent vasoconstrictor, thereby causing blood pressure to increase. Angiotensin II also causes the adrenal glands to release **aldosterone**, a hormone that stimulates the kidney to retain more sodium ions, and thus water, in the body.

Antidiuretic hormone (**ADH**) is released by the pituitary gland in response to rising plasma osmolality and/or a drop in blood volume or pressure. It, too, can activate the thirst center of the hypothalamus. Therefore, it is an important hormone concenring thirst regulation. Its name is derived from the word **diuresis**, which refers to increased urine production. Thus, ADH, an antidiuretic, is a hormone that inhibits urine formation and, in turn, helps prevent dehydration. ADH is also called vasopressin, reflecting its ability to constrict blood vessels. Interestingly, alcohol inhibits the release of ADH, thereby causing an increase in urine output. This helps explain why a person may have a dry mouth and feel thirsty the morning after excessive alcohol consumption—manifestations that reflect the dehydrating action of alcohol.

Long-term quenching of thirst depends on absorbing water from the small intestine, a process that lowers the osmolality of plasma. This, in turn, inhibits the thirst center and also causes saliva to form. However, it takes approximately 30 minutes for this process to take effect after we drink water. Obviously, it would be impractical if we had to drink for this length of time in order to feel satisfied. Fortunately, there are also short-term mechanisms that act more quickly to quench thirst.

Short-term thirst quenching of thirst occurs almost as soon as we begin to drink water, even though we have not had enough time to absorb this water into the bloodstream. It appears that simply moistening and cooling the membranes of the mouth and throat reduce the sensation of thirst. For instance, laboratory rats will drink less when their water is cool as compared with when it is warm. In addition, moistening a rat's mouth temporarily satisfies thirst even if this water is drained from the esophagus before it reaches the stomach.

Thirst is further satisfied when stretch receptors in the stomach and small intestine are stimulated because these receptors send signals to the thirst center. This proposed mechanism has been tested, for example, by allowing dogs to drink and then draining the water from the esophagus while the stomach is inflated with a balloon. It seems that simply stretching the stomach with an inanimate object is sufficient to help satisfy thirst.

Scientists believe that the "premature" dampening mechanisms of thirst described above keep us from drinking more than we need to and overdiluting our body fluids. However, these short-term mechanisms are effective for only about 30 to 45 minutes. In other words, if we do not actually get sufficient water into the bloodstream, the sensation of thirst soon returns. Only a drop in blood osmolality produces a long-lasting quenching of thirst.

REGULATION OF WATER OUTPUT

We cannot avoid losing certain amounts of water (obligatory water loss described above). This helps explain why we cannot survive for long without drinking. The only way to control water output significantly is through variations in urine volume. Although the mammalian kidney is well adapted to eliminate excess water and also to conserve water, the organ cannot prevent water loss. That is, humans have to flush some substances out of the body with water. In addition, it is important to note that the kidneys are not capable of replacing lost water. As a result, the kidneys do not restore fluid

YOUR HEALTH: THIRST

The sensation of thirst is an effective mechanism; however, it does not always reliably tell us how much water we need. For instance, during athletic events, we can satisfy our thirst by just drinking enough to cool our mouths and make them less dry. However, that does not mean we have drunk enough liquids to restore body fluid balance. In addition, elderly people may not recognize or pay attention to thirst signals. In contrast, some kidney or heart patients who are "fluid-overloaded" by intravenous injection may still feel thirsty.

volume during dehydration, but merely slow the rate of water loss until more water is ingested to restore balance.

The solute concentration (amount of dissolved substances) and volume of urine can vary quite a bit and depend on several factors, such as the amount of fluid intake, diet, and water loss by other means, such as perspiration. Normally, the kidneys begin to get rid of excess water about 30 minutes after it has been ingested, with most elimination taking place after about 60 minutes. This delay reflects the amount of time that it takes for water to be absorbed from the small intestine into the blood and to inhibit the release of antidiuretic hormone (ADH) from the pituitary gland, which causes the kidneys to produce a less concentrated, but more plentiful, urine. Conversely, if blood volume or pressure is too low, ADH release is stimulated, and urine output decreases in volume (Figure 10.2). This control of urine volume by ADH is an example of a negative feedback mechanism.

DISORDERS OF WATER BALANCE

Fluid deficiency occurs when water loss exceeds water intake over a long enough period of time. There are two kinds of deficiencies—volume depletion and dehydration—which differ in the relative loss of water and electrolytes (salts) and the resulting osmolality (concentration) of the extracellular fluid.

Volume depletion occurs when proportionate amounts of water and electrolytes (mostly sodium chloride) are lost without being replaced. This can happen, for instance, with excessive bleeding, severe burns, or chronic diarrhea and vomiting. In this case, the volume of total body water declines, but the osmolarity of body fluids remains normal.

In contrast, **dehydration** (negative water balance) occurs when the body loses a lot more water than it does electrolytes; therefore, the osmolarity of extracellular fluids increases. The most common cause of dehydration is a lack of drinking

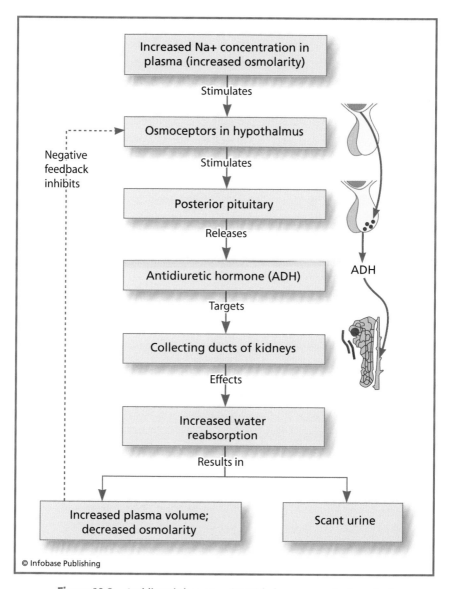

Figure 10.2 Antidiuretic hormone (ADH) helps conserve body water to make up for too much fluid output. Osmoreceptors in the hypothalamus monitor the concentration of dissolved substances in body fluids and trigger or inhibit the release of ADH as needed. Releasing ADH leads the kidneys to reabsorb water, thereby reducing the amount of urine expelled.

water—for instance, when someone is stranded at sea or in a desert. It also can be caused by an overuse of diuretics (agents that cause you to urinate), endocrine disorders (such as diabetes mellitus and diabetes insipidus), and prolonged exposure to cold weather. A serious consequence of severe dehydration is that the blood does not have a high enough plasma volume to circulate normally. This can lead to **hypovolemic shock**, a life-threatening condition in which the heart is unable to supply enough blood to the body.

YOUR HEALTH: DIABETES

The secretion of insufficient amounts of ADH (antidiuretic hormone) results in a disease called **diabetes insipidus**, which causes a person to excrete huge amounts of urine and suffer from intense thirst. *Diabetes* is a term that refers to "overflow," and *insipidus* means "tasteless." This disorder can be caused by a head injury that damages the hypothalamus or pituitary gland. Although it is certainly inconvenient, it is not usually life threatening, as long as the thirst center works normally and the person drinks enough water to prevent dehydration. However, diabetes insipidus can be fatal if the patient is unconscious or in a coma and does not get enough fluids. This is why doctors carefully monitor the urine flow of accident victims who have head trauma.

Diabetes mellitus also causes a large amount of urine output and thirst. However, it differs from diabetes insipidus because it is caused either by a failure of pancreatic cells to produce insulin (type I diabetes) or by the failure of the cells of the body to use insulin properly (type II diabetes). In addition, unlike the urine of people who have diabetes insipidus, the urine of individuals with diabetes mellitus contains glucose (*mel* means "honey"). These two disorders likely got their names from the way they were first diagnosed. In other words, at one time, health-care providers may have tasted a patient's urine or determined whether urine attracted insects in order to figure out the underlying cause of excessive urinary output.

It is also possible to have too much body fluid. However, this is not very common because when the osmolality of the extracellular fluid drops, ADH release is inhibited, allowing the kidneys to make up for excessive water intake by excreting more urine. Nonetheless, kidney failure or drinking far too much water in a short time period can cause excess fluid retention, or **hypotonic hydration** (also called *water intoxication*). This causes water to leak into tissue cells, making them swell as they become abnormally hydrated. Water intoxication is particularly damaging to neurons (nerve cells). If not treated, it can quickly lead to disorientation, convulsions, coma, and even death. It also causes excess fluid to accumulate in the lungs, inhibiting gas exchange. Water intoxication can be treated by intravenous injection with mannitol—a carbohydrate that remains in the extracellular fluid, which increases the osmolality of plasma, thereby helping draw water out of cells.

Fluid may also accumulate abnormally in a particular location of the body. In such a case, the total body water may be normal, but the volume of circulating blood may drop so low that the circulatory system collapses. The most common abnormal accumulation of fluid is called **edema**, in which fluid gathers in the interstitial spaces (spaces between cells), causing tissue to swell. This can be caused by increased blood pressure, localized blood blockage, congestive heart failure, or high blood volume. It also can occur when the walls of blood vessels become leaky and let too much fluid pass through, such as during an inflammatory response (e.g., edema occurs during an allergic response to a bee sting).

SENSE OF HUNGER

A person is said to be in energy balance if his or her energy content (calories) from food equals the amount of energy used by the body for muscular work and for the processes of metabolism plus heat loss. Excess food intake causes fat to be deposited, thereby increasing body weight. In contrast, a lack of food makes the body use fat deposits to do work. If this goes on for a long time, it can impair body function and eventually lead to death. We have the ability to adapt our food intake to changing needs, depending on the amount of physical activity, climate, and the nutritional value of the food we eat. In fact, the body weight of most people is amazingly stable because our bodies have ways to control food intake.

Hunger is a general sensation resulting from a lack of food, usually accompanied by the desire to eat. Like the sensation of thirst, its physiological mechanisms are not well understood. As we all know from experience, hunger occurs when the stomach is empty, and vanishes once the stomach is filled with food. It, therefore, seems apparent that hunger is stimulated, at least in part, by stomach peristalsis, or **hunger contractions**, which occur in a mild form soon after the stomach empties.

YOUR HEALTH: COLD WEATHER

Profuse sweating in hot weather is an obvious threat to fluid balance. However, physiological changes associated with cold weather can also cause fluid balance problems. When the body is very cold, it reduces heat loss by constricting blood vessels in tissues under the skin. This, in turn, raises blood pressure, inhibiting the release of antidiuretic hormone (ADH) and stimulating secretion of atrial natriuretic peptide (a hormone secreted by the heart in response to increased blood volume or pressure that acts on the kidneys to increase urinary output). Together, these changes lead to an increase in fluid loss from the body. In addition, cold air is relatively dry (it holds less moisture than warm air), which makes the body lose more water through breathing. As a result, prolonged exposure to cold weather can result in sufficient water loss to cause hypovolemia, a decrease in the volume of circulating blood. This helps explain why it is important to drink plenty of fluids when you take part in winter sports and other cold weather activities, such as shoveling snow.

These contractions get more intense over a period of hours, and they give us a powerful incentive to eat. However, other factors also influence appetite in ways similar to the mechanism of thirst. For instance, just chewing and swallowing food briefly satisfies appetite, even if the food is removed from the esophagus before it reaches the stomach. In addition, inflating the stomach with a balloon inhibits hunger, even if an animal has not actually swallowed any food.

As with thirst, the hypothalamus of the brain is involved with hunger feelings and satiety (a feeling of fullness or satisfaction). The **feeding center** of the hypothalamus is important for providing hunger sensations. For instance, when this part of the brain is destroyed in laboratory rats, they exhibit a loss of appetite and will starve to death if not force fed. In contrast, damage to the **satiety center** causes extreme overeating (**hyperphagia**), leading to **obesity**. It has been shown that the satiety center has **glucostats**—neurons that rapidly absorb blood glucose after a meal. Evidence indicates that when this occurs, the glucostats send inhibitory signals to the feeding center, thereby suppressing appetite (this has been termed the **glucostat hypothesis** of hunger). Some weight-loss drugs work by inhibiting the feeding center. As blood glucose levels drop between meals, inhibitory signals from the satiety center decline, allowing the feeding center to become more active, causing the sense of hunger to return.

A number of hormones also play a role in appetite regulation and feeding behavior. For instance, the hypothalamus produces a hormone called **neuropeptide Y**, which is a potent appetite stimulant and leads to a craving for carbohydrates. In contrast, the presence of amino acids and fatty acids in the small intestine stimulate cells to secrete a hormone called **cholecystokinin** (**CCK**), which acts as an appetite suppressant. Other chemicals produced in the body make us feel full and satisfied.

Interestingly, adipose cells (fat cells) can release a hormone called **leptin**, which circulates at levels related to the body's fat reserves. In fact, leptin levels are thought to serve as an indicator of the body's total energy stores and provide a way for the body to control hunger and long-term caloric intake. In addition, a number of studies indicate that the overall satiety signal is leptin, which is secreted over a period of hours exclusively by fat tissue in response to an increase in fatty mass in the body. Leptin acts on the hypothalamus and inhibits the secretion of neuropeptide Y, thereby suppressing appetite. Leptin also appears to inhibit **anandamide**, a chemical messenger that stimulates feeding, and a molecule that binds to the same receptors as tetrahydrocannibal, or THC, the active ingedient in marijuana.

As previously noted, scientists do not understand completely how the sense of hunger works. Most present-day studies are trying to determine the roles played by neural signals from the digestive tract, blood-borne signals related to body energy stores, hormones, body temperature (e.g., increased body temperature may inhibit eating), and psychological factors. Keep in mind that these mechanisms are not mutually exclusive, and most of these factors seem to operate through feedback signals to the feeding and satiety centers of the brain.

YOUR HEALTH: BMI

Obesity is defined as a body weight of more than 20% above what doctors recommend for a person's age, gender, and height. The National Institutes of Health (NIH) estimate that 50% of the people living in the United States today are overweight and 33% are clinically obese. The official measure of body weight is called the **body mass index** (**BMI**), an index of a person's weight relative to height. To estimate your BMI, multiply your weight in pounds by 705 and then divide by the square of your height in inches. A BMI of 20 to 25 is considered optimal for most people; a BMI over 27 is considered overweight and above 30 is considered obese.

CONNECTIONS

The feelings of thirst and hunger are not tied to a particular sense organ as the senses of vision and hearing are. As a result, they are often referred to as part of the general sensations. In order to remain properly hydrated, our water intake must equal our water output. Most water output is obligatory. Insensible water loss is one type of obligatory output, which occurs through our skin and when we breathe. Obligatory water output also occurs when we perspire, urinate, and defecate. Most of this water enters our body through ingested liquids. Additional water is obtained from solid foods, and metabolic water is produced by cellular metabolism.

Fluid intake is governed mainly by the sensation of thirst. Dehydration causes a reduction in blood volume and pressure, while also raising blood osmolality. Some of these changes are detected by the thirst center of the hypothalamus. The thirst center is stimulated when its osmoreceptor cells lose water through osmosis, which leads to a sensation of thirst and motivates us to drink.

The only way to control water output significantly is through variations in urine volume. Although the kidneys are well adapted to eliminate excess water and to conserve water, they cannot prevent water loss. Consequently, the kidneys do not restore fluid volume during dehydration, but instead slow the rate of water loss until more is ingested to restore balance. The solute concentration and volume of urine depend on several factors, including the amount of fluid intake, diet, and water loss by other avenues, such as perspiration.

Fluid deficiency occurs when water loss exceeds water intake over a sufficient period of time. Volume depletion occurs when proportionate amounts of water and electrolytes are lost without replacement. In contrast, dehydration (negative water balance) occurs when the body loses significantly more water than electrolytes, increasing the osmolality of extracellular fluids. The most common cause of dehydration

(continues)

(continued)

is a lack of drinking water, but it can also be caused by the overuse of diuretics, by endocrine disorders, and by prolonged exposure to cold weather.

It is possible to suffer from fluid excess. For instance, renal failure or drinking extraordinary amounts of water in a short time period can lead to excess fluid retention or hypotonic hydration. This condition promotes net osmosis of water into tissue cells, causing them to swell as they become abnormally hydrated. Fluid may also accumulate abnormally in a particular location. In edema, the most common form of abnormal fluid accumulation, fluid accumulates in the interstitial spaces, causing tissue to swell.

A person's energy balance is maintained in equilibrium if the energy content (calories) of food ingested equals the energy used for muscular work, metabolism, and heat loss. Physiological mechanisms control food intake. Lack of food causes the sensation of hunger, and subsequent food intake leads to satiety.

Hunger is a general sensation projected to the stomach region and is stimulated partly by stomach peristalsis (hunger contractions). As with thirst, the hypothalamus is involved with hunger sensations and satiety. The feeding center is important in providing hunger sensations, and the satiety center provides signals that let us know we are full. The satiety center has neurons called glucostats that send inhibitory signals to the feeding center, thereby suppressing appetite (glucostat hypothesis of hunger).

A number of hormones also play a role in appetite regulation and influence feeding behavior. Neuropeptide Y causes us to crave carbohydrates. In contrast, the hormone cholecystokinin (CCK) acts as an appetite suppressant. Adipose (fat) cells can release a hormone called leptin, which circulates at levels related to the body's fat reserves and appears to be the overall satiety signal.

Appendix: Conversion Chart

Unit (metric)	Metric to English	English to Metric
LENGTH		
Kilometer km	1 km 0.62 mile (mi)	1 mile (mi) 1.609 km
Meter m	1 m 3.28 feet (ft)	1 foot (ft) 0.305 m
Centimeter cm	1 cm 0.394 inches (in)	1 inch (in) 2.54 cm
Millimeter mm	1 mm 0.039 inches (in)	1 inch (in) 25.4 mm
Micrometer μm	1 - millionth of a meter	
WEIGHT (MASS)		
Kilogram kg	1 kg 2.2 pounds (lbs)	1 pound (lbs) 0.454 kg
Gram g	1 g 0.035 ounces (oz)	1 ounce (oz) 28.35 g
Milligram mg	1 mg 0.000035 ounces (oz)	
Microgram μg	1 - millionth of a gram	
VOLUME		
Liter L	1 L 1.06 quarts	1 gallon (gal) 3.785 L
		1 quart (qt) 0.94 L
		1 pint (pt) 0.47 L
Milliliter mL or cc	1 mL 0.034 fluid ounce (fl oz)	1 fluid ounce (fl oz) 29.57 mL
Microliter μL	1 - millionth of a liter	
TEMPERATURE		
	$[°C] = ([°F] - 32) \times 5/9$	$[°F] = [°C] \times 9/5 + 32$

Glossary

Accommodation   The ability of the lens of the eye to change its shape in order to keep the focal length constant.

Action potential   All-or-none electrical signal that is conducted along nerve axons.

Adaptation   A decrease in responsiveness during continued stimulation.

Adenylate cyclase   Enzyme that converts ATP to cyclic AMP (cAMP).

Ageusia   A condition in which individuals experience no sensation of taste.

Aldosterone   A hormone produced by the adrenal cortex that increases the reabsorption of sodium in the kidneys.

Amplitude   The height of periodic waves, such as sound waves.

Ampulla   A swollen sac at one end of a semicircular duct that contains sensory cells.

Amygdala   A structure in the brain; part of the limbic system that labels information to be remembered.

Analgesics   Drugs that act as painkillers.

Anandamide   An endogenous chemical messenger that stimulates feeding by binding to cannabinoid receptors in the brain.

Anosmia   Loss of the sense of smell.

Anterior cavity (of eye)   The smaller cavity in front of the lens of the eye filled with aqueous humor.

Anterior chamber (of eye)   Part of the anterior cavity of the eye located between the cornea and the iris.

Antidiuretic hormone (**ADH**);   A hormone secreted by the pituitary gland that reduces the flow of urine; also known as arginine vasopressin.

Aqueous humor   A transparent fluid that fills the anterior and posterior chambers of the eye.

Astigmatism   A defect in vision due to abnormal curvature of the cornea or lens.

Auditory tube   Passageway extending from the middle ear to the pharynx; the Eustachian tube.

Auricle   Portion of the outer ear composed of elastic cartilage covered with skin.

Autonomic   Occurring involuntarily.

Axon   Long, narrow extension of a nerve cell that conducts electrical signals called action potentials.

Baroreceptor   Receptor that responds to changes in pressure.

Basal cell   Cell of a taste bud that actively divides and differentiates into new supporting cells and sensory cells.

Basilar membrane   Membrane that separates the scala media from the scala tympani in the inner ear.

Bipolar cells   Cells in the retina that help perform preliminary processing and integration of visual information.

Blind spot   Area in the retina that lacks photoreceptors; the place where the optic nerve exits the eye.

Blue cone   Photoreceptor whose pigment responds maximally to wavelengths of light around 420 nm.

Body mass index (**BMI**)   Measure of body weight relative to a person's height.

Bony labyrinth   A maze of passageways in the ear containing the vestibule, the cochlea, and the semicircular canals.

Canal of Schlemm   Opening at the junction of the sclera and cornea of the eye that drains aqueous humor from the anterior chamber.

Cataract   A disease of the eye characterized by clouding of the lens.

Cerebral cortex   Integrating center in the brain for higher functions such as reasoning, speech, language, and imagination.

Cerumen   Soft, yellow-brown secretion found in the external ear canal;   earwax.

Ceruminous gland   Modified sweat gland in the auditory canal that produce cerumen (earwax).

Chemoreceptor Receptor cell that responds to chemicals in solution.

Cholecystokinin (CCK) Hormone secreted by the small intestine that acts as an appetite suppressant.

Choroid Highly vascular, deeply pigmented membrane of the tunica vasculosa of the eye.

Ciliary body Thickened part of the tunica vasculosa of the eye that consists of interlacing smooth muscle bundles that are important for controlling the lens shape.

Circumvallate papillae Largest of the lingual papillae; arranged in the shape of the letter "V" at the back of the tongue.

***cis*-retinal** Bent form of retinal when it is bound to opsin.

Cochlea A winding, snail-shaped tube of the bony labyrinth of the inner ear that contains the receptors for hearing.

Color blind An inability to see one or more colors, resulting from a lack of one or more of the cone types.

Complex receptors Localized collections of cells associated with the special sense organs.

Concave Curved like the interior of a circle or hollow sphere.

Conchae The three scroll-like ridges that project from the wall of the nasal cavity.

Conduction deafness Loss of hearing due to a hindrance in the conduction of sound to the fluids of the inner ear.

Cone Photoreceptor that operates in bright light and provides high-acuity color vision.

Conjunctiva An epithelium that covers the inner surface of the eyelids and the outer surface of the eye.

Conjunctivitis Inflammation of the conjunctiva resulting from irritation or infection.

Convex Evenly curved to resemble a segment of a sphere.

Cornea Transparent anterior portion of the tunica fibrosa of the eye.

Crista ampullaris Mound of hair cells and supporting cells within each ampulla of a semicircular duct; also called crista.

Cupula   Gelatinous region in a semicircular duct that extends from a crista to the roof of the ampulla.

Cyclic adenosine monophosphate (**cAMP**)   An intracellular messenger formed from ATP by the action of adenylate cyclase.

Dark adaptation   Changes that occur in light-adapted eyes in order for vision to occur in dim light.

Deafness   Any loss of hearing, regardless of cause.

Decibel (**dB**)   Unit for expressing the loudness of sound.

Dehydration   When the body loses significantly more water than electrolytes, so the osmolality of extracellular fluids increases.

Dendrite   Threadlike extension of a neuron (nerve cell) that conducts the nerve impulse toward the cell body.

Dermal papillae   Peglike projections of the dermis that extend into the epidermal layer; many contain the corpuscles involved in the sense of touch.

Diabetes insipidus   Disease characterized by excessive urination and thirst caused by inadequate secretion of antidiuretic hormone (ADH).

Diabetes mellitus   Disease resulting from inadequate production or utilization of insulin.

Diplopia   Double vision.

Drives   Motivational states that influence us to provide or obtain whatever the body feels is lacking.

Dynamic equilibrium   Sensory information about rotational movements of the head.

Dysgeusia   A condition in which an individual experiences a distortion of taste.

Edema   An abnormal accumulation of fluid in the interstitial spaces, causing swelling of tissues.

Electromagnetic energy   A form of energy that travels in space as waves and can be measured in photons.

Electromagnetic spectrum   The entire range of wavelengths or frequencies of electromagnetic energy.

Emmetropia   Condition in the eye in which parallel rays are focused precisely on the retina, making vision perfect.

Encapsulated nerve endings   One or more fiber terminals of sensory nerves enclosed in a connective tissue capsule.

Endolymph   Fluid within the membranous labyrinth of the inner ear.

Equilibrium   State of balance.

External auditory canal   Passageway leading from the outer ear to the eardrum.

Exteroceptor   Receptor that responds to stimuli arising outside the body.

Extrinsic eye muscle   Muscle attached directly to the external surface of the eyeball and the wall of the orbit.

Eyebrow   Short, coarse hairs that overlie the supraorbital margins of the skull.

Eyelid   Movable fold of skin over the eye.

Fast pain   An initial feeling of sharp, localized, stabbing pain perceived at the time of an injury.

Feeding center   Region in the hypothalamus that leads to the sensation of hunger when stimulated.

Fight-or-flight response   A reaction in which the body becomes alarmed when confronted by an external stimulus and prepares either to defend itself against the source of the stimulation or to run away from the perceived threat.

Filiform papillae   Tiny bumps that cover the surface of the tongue; they lack taste buds.

Focal distance   Distance between the center of a lens and its focal point.

Focal length   See *Focal distance.*

Focal point   A single spot on the retina where focused light rays converge.

Foliate papillae   Folds along the back edges of the tongue that are well developed in children but less prominent and numerous in adults.

Fovea centralis   Location in the retina that contains only cones; functions for most acute vision.

Frequency   The number of waves that pass a given point over a period of time.

Fungiform papillae   Mushroom-shaped structures scattered over the entire surface of the tongue.

Ganglion cells   Cells in the retina that generate action potentials.

General senses   Senses that include touch, pressure, stretch, vibration, temperature monitoring (heat and cold), and pain.

Glands of Zeis   Small sebaceous glands associated with eyelash follicles.

Glaucoma   Disease of the eye characterized by an increase in intraocular pressure resulting from reduced drainage of aqueous humor.

Glomeruli   Complex spherical structures in the olfactory bulb.

Glucostat   Neuron in the satiety center that absorbs glucose after a meal.

Glucostat hypothesis   The idea that glucostats send inhibitory signals to the feeding center after a meal, thereby suppressing appetite.

Golgi tendon organ   Proprioceptor located in tendons that monitors tension produced during muscular contraction.

Granule cells   Cells of the olfactory bulb that inhibit the activity of mitral cells.

Green cone   Photoreceptor whose pigment responds maximally to wavelengths of light around 530 nm.

Gustation   The sense of taste.

Gustatory cell   Receptor cell for taste.

Hair cell   Epithelial cell of the organ of Corti that is topped with stereocilia.

Hertz (Hz)   Number of cycles of a wave per second.

Hunger   Sensation resulting from a lack of food, usually accompanied by the desire to eat.

Hunger contraction   Muscular contraction in the normal empty stomach.

Hyperopia   Defect in vision in which light rays come to a focus behind the retina; farsightedness.

Hyperphagia   Extreme overeating, which leads to obesity.

Hypogeusia   Condition where the threshold (minimum concentration) for taste perception is above the normal range, making it harder to taste substances.

Hypothalamus   Major control center in the brain for the body's autonomic functions.

Hypotonic hydration   Excess fluid retention that can be caused by kidney failure or drinking an extraordinary amount of water in a short time period.

Hypovolemic shock   Condition in which rapid fluid loss causes multiple organ failure.

Incus   Middle ear bone resembling an anvil in shape.

Inferior meatus   A horizontal passageway along the lateral wall of the nasal cavity.

Inner ear   The bony labyrinth and a series of fluid-filled membranous sacs and ducts contained within it (the membranous labyrinth).

Inner hair cell   Receptor cell for hearing; converts sound energy into electrical signals.

Inner segment   Region of a photoreceptor that corresponds to the cell body of a nerve cell.

Insensible water loss   Water loss through the skin and from breathing; water loss that is not usually noticed.

Interoceptor   Receptor that detects stimuli arising within the body, such as those from the internal organs and blood vessels.

Iris   Visible colored part of the eye suspended between the cornea and the lens.

Ischemia   Deficient blood flow to a specific body region or part.

Juxtaglomerular apparatus   Specialized cells in the kidneys that respond to a drop in blood pressure (or blood volume) or plasma solute concentration by releasing renin.

Kinocilium   A true cilium on the surface of hair cells.

Krause end bulb   Touch receptor found in mucous membranes.

Labeled line code   Nerve tracts that deliver sensory information to specific regions of the brain.

Lacrimal apparatus   Structures responsible for the production, distribution, and removal of tears.

Lacrimal canals   Tiny tubes that connect the lacrimal puncta to the lacrimal sac.

Lacrimal caruncle   Soft tissue mass that contains sebaceous and sweat glands, located on the conjunctiva near the medial commissure.

Lacrimal gland   Structure that secretes tears.

Lacrimal puncta   Tiny openings that drain tears from the eye.

Lacrimal sac   Upper dilated portion of the nasolacrimal duct.

Lacrimal secretion   A dilute saline solution; tears.

Lateral commissures   The point where the two eyelids meet at the lateral side of the eye.

Lens   Transparent, flexible structure that can change its shape to allow for precise focusing of light on the retina.

Leptin   Hormone released by fat cells that acts on the hypothalamus and inhibits the secretion of neuropeptide Y, thereby suppressing appetite.

Light adaptation   Changes that occur in dark-adapted eyes in order for vision to occur in bright light.

Limbic system   Part of the brain, including the amygdala and hypothalamus, that plays an important role in feeling emotions.

Lingual papillae   Peglike projections that give the tongue a slightly rough feel.

Lobule   The earlobe.

Loudness   The perception of sound energy; the pressure difference between the compressed and rarefied areas.

Lysozyme   An enzyme found in tears that has antibacterial properties.

Maculae   Anatomical structures that take the form of "spots" that differentiate them from the surrounding structures..

Macula lutea   Retinal region that contains mostly cones.

Macula sacculi   Sensory receptors for static equilibrium situated nearly vertically in the wall of the saccule.

Macula utriculi   Sensory receptors for static equilibrium situated nearly horizontally on the floor of the utricle.

Malleus   Middle ear bone resembling a hammer, attached to the eardrum.

Mechanoreceptor   Receptor cell that responds to physical deformation caused by touch, pressure, stretch, tension, or vibration.

Medial commissure   The point where the two eyelids meet near the bridge of the nose.

Meibomian gland   One of the sebaceous glands between the tarsi and conjunctiva of eyelids.

Meissner's corpuscle   Phasic receptor in the skin that senses light touch and texture.

Membranous labyrinth   Series of fluid-filled membranous sacs and ducts contained within the bony labyrinth.

Merkel's disk   Tonic receptor in the skin that senses light touch.

Metabolic water   Water produced in the body through cellular metabolism.

Middle ear   Small, air-filled space located in the tympanic cavity of the temporal bone.

Mitral cell   Second-order neuron that transmits impulses from an olfactory bulb to destinations within the brain via the olfactory tracts.

Modality   Type of sensation produced by a stimulus.

Motion sickness   An equilibrium disorder leading to symptoms of sweating, pallor, nausea, and vomiting.

Muscle spindle   Proprioceptor found throughout skeletal muscles that respond to muscle stretch.

Myelin sheath   Insulating layer that is produced by Schwann cells and surrounds nerve axons.

Myopia   Defect in vision in which light rays come to a focus in front of the retina; nearsightedness.

Nasal cavity   Space between the roof of the mouth and the floor of the skull.

Nasal septum   The partition dividing the nasal cavity into two spaces, left and right.

Nasolacrimal duct   Duct that drains tears from the lacrimal sac to the nasal cavity.

Neuron   Nerve cell; capable of conducting electrical signals.

Neuropeptide Y   Hypothalamic hormone that acts as a potent appetite stimulant.

Night blindness   Inability to see well in dim light or in darkness; defect in vision due to a lack of rhodopsin in the rods.

Nociceptor   Receptor that responds to potentially damaging stimuli and causes pain.

Obesity   A condition in which an individual is extremely overweight.

Olfaction   The sense of smell.

Olfactory bulb   The distal end of the olfactory tract, which is composed mainly of mitral cell axons.

Olfactory cell   Receptor cell for the sense of smell.

Olfactory cilia   Microvilli on the surface of olfactory cells.

Olfactory epithelium   Small region in the nasal cavity that contains olfactory cells, basal cells, and supporting cells.

Olfactory gland   Mucus-producing cell of the connective tissue underlying the olfactory epithelium.

Olfactory nerve   Sensory nerve that runs from the nasal cavity to the olfactory bulbs.

Olfactory region   Small, yellow-tinged region in the nasal cavity containing 10 million to 20 million olfactory cells.

Olfactory tracts   Axons of mitral cells that transmit signals from olfactory bulbs to other parts of the brain.

Opsin   Protein that combines with retinal to form visual pigment.

Optic disk   Area in the retina where the optic nerve exits the eye to form the optic nerve; also called the blind spot.

Optic nerve   Nerve that carries impulses for the sense of sight.

Orbit   Bony cavity in the frontal bone of the skull that holds and protects the eyeball.

Organ of Corti   Receptor organ for the sense of hearing.

Osmoreceptor   Cell that depolarizes in response to a loss of water by osmosis.

Ossicles   The three small bones of the middle ear.

Otitis media   A middle ear inflammation.

Otolith   Tiny calcium carbonate crystals in the otolithic membrane.

Otolithic membrane   Gelatinous membrane covering the hair cells of macula sacculi and macula utriculi.

Otosclerosis   Loss of hearing due to overgrowth of bony tissue that fuses the stapes to the oval window or fuses the ossicles to one another.

Outer ear   Portion of the ear composed of the external ear (auricle and lobule) and the external auditory canal.

Outer hair cell   Cell that adjusts the response of the cochlea to different frequencies, enabling the inner hair cells to work with greater precision.

Outer segment   Receptor region of a photoreceptor.

Oval window   Oval aperture between the middle and inner ear into which the base of the stapes fits.

Pacinian corpuscle   Phasic receptor in the skin that senses deep pressure, stretch, tickle, and vibration.

Palpebral fissure   The opening between the eyelids.

Perception   Assigning meaning to a sensation based on experience.

Perilymph   Fluid between the bony labyrinth and the membranous labyrinth of the inner ear.

Phantom pain   Perception of feeling or pain in a limb after it has been surgically amputated.

Phasic receptors   Receptors that generate a burst of activity when first stimulated and then quickly stop transmitting impulses even if the stimulus continues.

Pheromone   A chemical secreted by the body that travels through the air and can influence the physiology of another individual.

Photochemical reaction   A reaction in which the chemical structure of a molecule is changed by interaction with light energy.

Photon   Discrete unit of energy of light.

Photoreception   Conversion of light energy to chemical energy by receptors in the retina of the eye.

Photoreceptor   Receptor cell that responds to light energy.

Pigmented layer   Outer, single-cell-thick layer of the sensory tunic of the eye.

Pitch   The sense of whether a sound is high or low; determined by the frequency of sound waves.

Posterior cavity (of eye)   Large cavity behind the lens and ciliary body containing vitreous humor.

Posterior chamber (of eye)   Part of the anterior cavity located between the iris and lens.

Presbyopia   Defect in vision resulting from advancing age that involves the loss of the ability of the lens to change its shape (accommodate), inhibiting close vision.

Proprioceptor   Receptor located in skeletal muscles, tendons, and joints that is important for sensing the position and movements of the body and its parts.

Prostaglandins   A group of fatty acids that are secreted by body tissues and serve as sensory messengers.

Pupil   The adjustable, central opening of the iris.

Pupillary reflex   Constriction of the pupils in response to light illuminating the eyes.

Receptor potential   Graded change in the voltage across a receptor cell membrane in response to a stimulus.

Receptor specificity   The concept of receptors responding to specific kinds of stimuli.

Red cone   Photoreceptor whose pigment responds maximally to wavelengths of light around 565 nm.

Referred pain   Projection by the brain that may cause visceral pain to be perceived as somatic in origin.

Refraction   Bending of light rays as they pass obliquely through media of different densities.

Refractive index   Measure of how much a medium refracts light rays relative to air.

Retina   Inner layer of the sensory tunic that contains photoreceptors.

Retinal   Light-absorbing molecule that is formed from vitamin A.

Retinal detachment   Disorder characterized by separation of the retina from the pigmented layer, which allows the jellylike vitreous humor to seep between them.

Retinopathy   Disease of the retina.

Rhodopsin   Visual pigment in the outer segment of retinal rods.

Rod   Photoreceptor for vision that functions in dim light and for peripheral vision.

Root hair plexus   Unencapsulated nerve ending that monitors the movement of hairs by wrapping around hair follicles.

Round window   Membrane separating the middle ear from the inner ear.

Ruffini's corpuscle   Tonic receptor for heavy touch, pressure, stretching of the skin, and joint movements.

Saccade   Small, jerky movements that quickly move the eye from one location to another.

Saccule   Anterior chamber of the vestibular apparatus used for sensing the position of the head in space.

Satiety center   A region in the hypothalamus that leads to the sensation of fullness and satiation when stimulated.

Scala media   Chamber of the cochlea located between the scala tympani and scala vestibuli that houses the organ of Corti; filled with endolymph.

Scala tympani   Inferior chamber of the cochlea; filled with perilymph.

Scala vestibuli   Superior chamber of the cochlea; filled with perilymph.

Scanning movements   Eye movements that track a moving object.

Schwann cell   Cell that forms the myelin sheath, the insulating layer around nerve fibers.

Sclera   Tough, white, fibrous tissue of the tunic fibrosa; covers most of the outer surface of the eye.

Semicircular canal   Bony canal in the temporal bone containing a semicircular duct.

Semicircular duct   Part of the vestibular apparatus that senses rotational movements of the head.

Sensation   The awareness and localization of a stimulus.

Sense organ   Localized collection of cells associated with a special sense.

Sensorineural deafness   Loss of hearing due to damage of neural structures.

Sensory neuron   A nerve that transmits signals from receptors to the central nervous system.

Sensory projection   Ability to identify the site of stimulation based on information carried by nerve fibers.

Sensory reception   Detection of stimulus energy by sensory receptor cells.

Sensory receptor   Anatomical structure composed of sensory cells that is specialized to respond to specific changes in the environment.

Sensory tunic   Innermost layer of the eye.

Serous glands   Glands of the mouth, associated with taste buds, that produce a thin, watery secretion.

Simple receptor   Receptor composed of the modified endings (dendrites) of a sensory nerve.

Slow pain   A long-lasting, dull, diffuse feeling of pain following an injury.

Somatic pain   Pain that arises from the skin, muscles, or joints.

Sound   Any audible vibration of molecules.

Sound wave   Series of pressure disturbances consisting of alternating compressions and rarefactions.

Special sense   Any of the senses of hearing, balance, smell, vision, or taste.

Spectrum   A band of colors seen when light passes through a prism.

Stapedius   A small muscle of the middle ear connected to the stapes.

Stapes   Middle ear bone resembling a stirrup in shape; attached to the oval window.

Static equilibrium   Sensory information about one's position in space with respect to gravity.

Stereocilia   Long, stiff microvilli on the surface of hair cells.

Stimulus   A change in the internal or external environment that evokes a response.

Strabismus   A disorder where the two eyes cannot focus on the same object.

Sty   An inflammatory swelling of a sebaceous gland in the eyelid caused by a bacterial infection.

Supporting cell   Cell in a taste bud that helps insulate sensory cells.

Suspensory ligament   In the eye, ring of fibers attached to the ciliary body, which suspends the lens.

Tarsal plate   A sheet of supporting connective tissue in the eyelid.

Taste bud   Sensory structure composed of specialized epithelial cells that mediate the sensation of taste.

Taste hairs   Microvilli on the apical surface of taste cells.

Taste pore   Fluid-filled space over a taste bud.

Tectorial membrane   An anchored, gelatinous covering over the organ of Corti.

Tensor tympani   A small muscle of the middle ear connected to the malleus.

Thalamus   An integrating, filtering, and relay center in the brain.

Thermoreceptor   Receptor cell that responds to changes in temperature.

Thirst   Desire for fluid, especially water.

Thirst center   Region in the hypothalamus that leads to the sensation of thirst when stimulated.

Tinnitus   A ringing or clicking sound in the ears in the absence of auditory stimuli.

Tonic receptors   Receptors that adapt slowly and therefore generate nerve impulses continually.

Transduction   Translation of a stimulus into an electrical signal by sensory receptor cells.

***trans*-retinal**   The straight form of retinal induced by the absorption of light.

Tunica fibrosa   Outermost layer of the eyeball.

Tunica vasculosa   Middle layer of the eye.

Tympanic cavity   The indentation in the temporal bone that houses the structures of the middle ear.

Tympanic membrane   A membrane separating the outer and middle ears; the eardrum.

Unencapsulated nerve endings   General sensory receptors that are not wrapped in connective tissue.

Utricle   Posterior chamber of the vestibular apparatus; functions in sensing the position of the head in space.

Vestibular apparatus   Structure of the inner ear that contains receptors for the sense of equilibrium.

Vestibular membrane   A membrane that separates the scala media from the scala vestibuli in the inner ear.

Visceral pain   Pain from noxious stimulation of receptors in the organs of the thorax and abdominal cavity.

Visible light   Region of the electromagnetic spectrum with wavelengths between about 400 and 700 nm.

Vision   The perception of objects in the environment by means of the light that they emit or reflect.

Visual acuity   Measure of the resolving power of the eye rated against a standard in which a person with normal sight is considered to have 20/20 vision.

Visual pigment   Photopigment in photoreceptors that changes shape when it absorbs light.

Vitreous humor   Transparent jellylike substance that fills the posterior chamber of the eye.

Volume depletion   Fluid deficiency in which proportionate amounts of water and electrolytes are lost without replacement, as during hemorrhage or chronic diarrhea.

Wavelength   Distance between two consecutive wave crests or troughs.

Bibliography

Books and Journals

Bard, A., and M. Bard. "The Complete Idiot's Guide to Understanding the Brain." New York: Penguin Group USA. 2002. 360.

Baylor, D. "How Photons Start Vision." *Proceedings of the National Academy of Sciences of the United States of America* 93 (1996): 560–565.

Borg, E., and S.A. Counter. "The Middle-Ear Muscles." *Scientific American* 261 (1989): 74–80.

Byrne, J.H., and S.G. Schultz. *Introduction to Membrane Transport and Bioelectricity: Foundations of General Physiology and Electrochemical Signaling.* New York: Raven Press. 1994. 208.

Campbell, N., and J.B. Reece. *Biology.* 7th ed. San Francisco: Benjamin Cummings. 2004. 1312.

Fain, G.L. *Sensory Transduction.* Sunderland, MA: Sinauer Associates. 2003. 288.

French, A.S., and P.H. Torkkeli. "The Basis of Rapid Adaptation in Mechanoreceptors." *News in Physiological Science* 9 (1994): 158–161.

Herness, M.S., and T.A. Gilbertson. "Cellular Mechanisms of Taste Transduction." *Annual Review of Physiology* 61 (1999): 873–900.

Holloway, M. "The Ascent of Scent." *Scientific American* 281 (1999): 42–44.

Hudspeth, A.J. "The Hair Cells of the Inner Ear." *Scientific American* 248 (1983): 54–64.

———. "How the Ear's Works Work." *Nature* 341 (1989): 397–404.

Kandel, E.R., J.H. Schwartz, and T.M. Jessell. *Principles of Neural Science,* 4th ed. New York: McGraw-Hill. 2000. 1414.

Kinnamon, S.C., and T.A. Cummings. "Chemosensory Transduction Mechanisms in Taste." *Annual Review of Physiology* 54 (1992): 715–731.

Koretz, J.F., and G.H. Handelman. "How the Human Eye Focuses." *Scientific American* 259 (1988): 92–99.

Lindemann, B. "Receptors and Transduction in Taste." *Nature* 413 (2001): 219–225.

McLaughlin, S., and R.F. Margolskee. "The Sense of Taste." *American Scientist* 82 (1994): 538–545.

Purves, D., G.J. Augustine, D. Fitzpatrick, L.C. Katz, A.S. LaMantia, J.O. McNamara, and S.M. Williams. *Neuroscience*. 4th ed. Sunderland, MA: Sinauer Associates. 2008. 857.

Schnapf, J.L., and D.A. Baylor. "How Photoreceptor Cells Respond to Light." *Scientific American* 256 (1987): 40–47.

Sheperd, G.M. *Synaptic Organization of the Brain*, 4th ed. New York: Oxford University Press. 1997. 656.

Smith, D.V., and R.F. Margolskee. "Making Sense of Taste." *Scientific American* 284 (2001): 32–39.

Squire, L.J. Roberts, N. Spitzer, M. Zigmond, S. McConnell, and F. Bloom. *Fundamental Neuroscience*, 2nd ed. New York: Academic Press. 2002. 1426.

Stryer, L., J.M. Berg, and J.L. Tymoczko. *Biochemistry*, 5th ed. San Francisco: W.H. Freeman & Co. 2002. 1100.

———. "The Molecules of Visual Excitation." *Scientific American* 257 (1987): 42–50.

Torre, V., J.F. Ashmore, T.D. Lamb, and A. Menine. "Transduction and Adaptation in Sensory Receptor Cells." *The Journal of Neuroscience* 15 (1995): 7757–7768.

Wassle, H., and B.B. Boycott. "Functional Architecture of the Mammalian Retina." *Physiological Reviews* 71 (1991): 447–480.

Web Sites

Antidiuretic Hormone

http://www.vivo.colostate.edu/hbooks/pathphys/endocrine/ hypopit/adh.html

Balance Disorders

http://www.nidcd.nih.gov/health/balance/balance_disor-ders.asp

Cataract

http://www.nei.nih.gov/health/cataract/cataract_facts.htm

Chemoreceptors

http://www.cals.ncsu.edu/course/ent425/tutorial/chemo.html

Color Vision in Animals

http://www.learner.org/channel/workshops/sheddinglight/highlights/highlights4a.html

Electromagnetic Spectrum

http://csep10.phys.utk.edu/astr162/lect/light/spectrum.html

Eye Structure and Function

http://retina.anatomy.upenn.edu/~lance/eye/eye.html

Genetics of Eye Color

http://seps.mgd-colo.peak.org/cvoracle/faq/eyecolor.html

Glaucoma

http://www.nei.nih.gov/health/glaucoma/glaucoma_facts.htm

Introduction to Sensory Receptors

http://www.zoology.ubc.ca/~auld/bio350/lectures/sensory_receptors.html

Limbic System

http://thalamus.wustl.edu/course/limbic.html

Mechanoreceptors

http://users.rcn.com/jkimball.ma.ultranet/BiologyPages/M/Mechanoreceptors.html

Pain

http://webspace.ship.edu/cgboer/pain.html

Photon

http://physics.about.com/od/lightoptics/f/photon.htm

Presbyopia

http://www.aoa.org/x4697.xml

Sensation and Perception

*http://www.audiblox2000.com/learning_disabilities/
sensation.htm*

Sense of Hearing

*http://www1.omi.tulane.edu/departments/pathology/fer-
min/Hearing.html*

Sense of Smell

*http://users.rcn.com/jkimball.ma.ultranet/BiologyPages/O/
Olfaction.html*

Sense of Taste

*http://users.rcn.com/jkimball.ma.ultranet/BiologyPages/T/
Taste.html*

Sensory Physiology

http://fig.cox.miami.edu/~cmallery/150/neuro/senses.htm

Sensory Receptor Physiology

*http://www.unm.edu/~toolson/Receptor_Function_
Handout.html*

Sensory Systems

*http://faculty.clintoncc.suny.edu/faculty/michael.
gregory/files/bio%20102/bio%20102%20lectures/
sensory%20systems/sensory.htm*

Structure and Function of Cell Membranes

*http://users.rcn.com/jkimball.ma.ultranet/BiologyPages/C/
CellMembranes.html*

Taste Receptors

*http://www.zoology.ubc.ca/~auld/bio350/lectures/sensory_
taste.html*

Further Resources

Books and Journals

Axel, R. "The Molecular Logic of Smell." *Scientific American* 273 (1995): 154–159.

Barlow, R.B. "What the Brain Tells the Eye." *Scientific American* 262 (1990): 90–95.

Buck, L.B. "The Molecular Architecture of Odor and Pheromone Sensing in Mammals." *Cell* 100 (2000): 611–618.

Chiras, D.D. *Human Biology.* 5th ed. Boston: Jones and Bartlett Publishers. 2005. 464.

Eatock, R.A. "Adaptation in Hair Cells" *Annual Review of Neuroscience* 23 (2000): 285–314.

Fain, G.L., H.R. Matthews, M.C. Cornwall, and Y. Koutalos. "Adaptation in Vertebrate Photoreceptors." *Physiological Review* 81 (2001): 117–151.

Fettiplace, R., and P.A. Fuchs. "Mechanisms of Hair Cell Tuning." *Annual Review of Physiology* 61 (1999): 809–834.

Gilbertson, T.A., S. Damak, and R.F. Margolskee. "The Molecular Physiology of Taste Transduction." *Current Opinion in Neurobiology* 10 (2000): 519–527.

Gillespie, P.G., and R.G. Walker. "Molecular Basis of Mechanosensory Transduction." *Nature* 413 (2001): 194–202.

Hamann, W. "Mammalian Cutaneous Mechanoreceptors." *Progress in Biophysics and Molecular Biology* 64 (1995): 81–104.

Hille, B. *Ionic Channels of Excitable Membranes*, 3rd ed., Sunderland, MA: Sinauer Associates. 2001. 814.

Holloway, M. "Seeing the Cells that See." *Scientific American* 272 (1995): 27.

Illy, E. "The Complexity of Coffee." *Scientific American* 286 (2002): 86–91.

Johnson, M.D. *Human Biology: Concepts and Current Issues.* 3rd ed. San Francisco: Benjamin Cummings. (2005) 592.

Julius, D., and A.I. Basbaum. "Molecular Mechanisms of Nociception." *Nature* 413 (2001): 203–210.

Kalat, J.W. *Introduction to Psychology.* 8th ed. Belmont, CA: Wadsworth. 2007. 768.

Lent, C.M., and M.H. Dickinson. "The Neurobiology of Feeding in Leeches." *Scientific American* 258 (1988): 98–103.

Lindemann, B. "Taste Reception." *Physiological Reviews* 76 (3) (1996): 718–766.

Livingstone, M.S. "Art, Illusion, and the Visual System." *Scientific American* 258 (1988): 78–85.

Mambaerts, P. "Seven-Transmembrane Proteins as Odorant and Chemosensory Receptors." *Science* 2886 (1999): 707–711.

Marieb, E and K.N. Hoehn. *Human Anatomy and Physiology.* 7th ed. San Francisco: Benjamin Cummings. 2006. 1159.

Martin, A., B. Wallace, P. Fuchs, J. Nicholls. "From Neuron to Brain: A Cellular and Molecular Approach to the Function of the Nervous System." 4th ed. Sinauer Associates. 2001. 679.

Martini, F.H. *Fundamentals of Anatomy and Physiology.* 7th ed. San Francisco: Benjamin Cummings. 2005. 1248.

Murakami, M., and H. Kijimia. "Transduction Ion Channels Directly Gated by Sugars on the Insect Taste Cell." *The Journal of General Physiology* 115. 2000. 455–466.

Nef, P. "How We Smell: The Molecular and Cellular Bases of Olfaction." *News in Physiological Science* 13 (1998): 1–5.

Neher, E., and B. Sakmann. "The Patch Clamp Technique." *Scientific American* 266 (1992): 44–51.

Nobili, R., F. Mammano, and J. Ashmore. "How Well Do We Understand the Cochlea?" *Trends in Neuroscience* 21 (1998): 159–167.

Pfenning, D.W., and P.W. Sherman. "Kin Recognition." *Scientific American* 272 (1995): 98–103.

Ramachandran, V.S. "Blind Spots." *Scientific American* 266 (1992): 86–91.

Saladin, K. *Anatomy and Physiology: The Unity of Form and Function*, 4th ed. New York: McGraw Hill. 2007. 1180.

Shier, D., J. Butler, and R. Lewis. *Hole's Essentials of Human Anatomy and Physiology*, 9th ed. Boston: McGraw Hill. 2005. 617.

Sun, H., and J. Nathans. "The Challenge of Macular Degeneration." *Scientific American* 285 (2001): 68–75.

Web Sites

American Diabetes Association
http://www.diabetes.org/homepage.jsp

Blind Spots
http://serendip.brynmawr.edu/bb/blindspot1.html

Body Mass Index Calculator
http://www.cdc.gov/nccdphp/dnpa/bmi/calc-bmi.htm

The Chemistry of Smelling
http://www.schoolscience.co.uk/content/5/chemistry/smells/smellsch2pg1.html

Chronic Pain
http://www.painrecoveryonline.com/aamaslides_files/frame.htm

Color Blindness
http://colorvisiontesting.com/

Corneal Transplant
http://www.opt.indiana.edu/lowther/html/keratoconus_transplant.htm

Dogs Smell Cancer in Patients
http://www.sciencedaily.com/releases/2006/01/060106002944.htm

Ear Tubes

http://aao-hns.org/healthinfo/ears/Ear-Tubes.cfm

Evolution of Color Vision

http://www.talkorigins.org/faqs/vision.html

General Anesthesia

*http://www.google.com/search?hl=en&q=general+anesthesi
a&btnG=Google+Search*

General Senses Versus the Special Senses

*http://krupp.wcc.hawaii.edu/BIOL100/present/senses/
sld002.htm*

Hansen's Disease

http://www.essortment.com/all/hansensdisease_rltp.htm

Human Sense of Smell

http://www.sirc.org/publik/smell_human.html

Inner Ear Primer

*http://www.mcl.tulane.edu/departments/pathology/fermin/
InnerEarPrimer.html*

Inner Ear Infections

*http://www.formulamedical.com/Topics/Head&Neck/inner
%20ear%20infection%20labyrinthitis.htm*

Ion Channels and Membrane Transport

http://www.omedon.co.uk/ionchan

Ishihara Test for Color Blindness

http://www.toledo-bend.com/colorblind/Ishihara.html

Membrane Structure and Transport

*http://www.emc.maricopa.edu/faculty/farabee/BIOBK/
BioBooktransp.html*

Motion Sickness

http://www.medicinenet.com/motion_sickness/article.htm

Myopia

http://www.oregoneyecenter.com/myopia.htm

Nictitating Membrane

http://www.wisegeek.com/what-is-a-nictitating-membrane.
htm

Night Blindness

http://members.tripod.com/manisha_b/Retina/RP.htm

Otosclerosis

http://www.nidcd.nih.gov/health/hearing/otosclerosis.asp

Phantom Limb Pain

http://www.mayoclinic.
com/health/phantom-pain/DS00444

Photoreceptors

http://www.cquest.utoronto.ca/psych/psy280f/ch2/photorecep-
tors.html

Properties of Light

http://theory.uwinnipeg.ca/mod_tech/node110.html

Renin-Angiotensin System

http://highbloodpressure.about.com/od/highbloodpres-
sure101/a/renin-system.htm

Tapetum Lucidum

http://www.ncbi.nlm.nih.gov/pubmed/14738502

Scratch Reflex

*http://www.scholarshipsinindia.com/answer/scratch_*
reflex.html

Sensation and Perception Tutorials

http://psych.hanover.edu/Krantz/sen_tut.html

Smell

http://www.cf.ac.uk/biosi/staff/jacob/teaching/sensory/olfact1.
html

Water Intoxication

http://chemistry.about.com/cs/5/f/blwaterintox.htm

What Causes the Smell after Rain

http://science.howstuffworks.com/question479.htm

Why Does Scratching Relieve an Itch

http://www.sciencedaily.com/releases/2008/01/08013112180
4.htm

Picture Credits

Page

Index

A

accommodation, 84
action potentials, 49
adaptation, 19–20, 53, 90–92
adenylate cyclase, 52
ADH. *See* antidiuretic hormone (ADH)
adipose cells in hunger regulation, 127–128
age-related changes
   in olfaction, 52
   in taste, 34, 40
   in vision, 74, 76, 84
ageusia, 42
aldosterone, 119
alkaline (soapy) taste, 39
amplitude, 96
ampulla, 113
amygdala, 53
analgesics, 18
anandamide, 128
anesthetics, general, 18
angiotensin II, 119
anosmia, 51
anterior cavity (eye), 74–75
anterior chamber, 74
antidiuretic hormone (ADH), 120, 122, 124
appetite. *See* hunger
aqueous humor, 69, 74–75
Aristotle, 15
astigmatism, 82
auditory canal, external (ear canal), 97
auditory tube, 98
auricle (pinna), 97
autonomic regulation, 25
axon, 49

B

balance. *See* equilibrium
baroreceptors, 25
basal cells, 36, 47
basilar membrane, 101, 106
bipolar cells (retina), 70
bitter taste, 38, 39
bleaching, 87–89
blind spot, 70
blindness. *See* vision loss
blood pressure control, 25
blue cones, 89
body mass index (BMI), 128
body water, total, 117
bony labyrinth, 100
brain. *See also* hypothalamus
   olfactory pathways, 53–54
   sensory input and, 10–11, 13, 15
   sensory projection, 18–19
   and taste perception, 42
brain surgery, 13, 15
breathing regulation, 25

C

cAMP (cyclic adenosine monophosphate), 52
canal of Schlemm, 75
cancer, dogs in detection of, 46
cataracts, 74
CCK (cholecystokinin), 127
cerebral cortex, 10, 54–55
cerumen, 97
ceruminous glands, 97
chemoreceptors, 15, 25, 34, 41, 42, 45
cholecystokinin (CCK), 127
choroid, 68–69
cilia, 49, 51

ciliary body, 69
circumvallate papillae, 35
cis-retinal, 87–88
close vision, 84
cochlea, 101
cold perception, 22–23
cold weather, fluid loss in, 126
color blindness, 91
color vision, 87, 89, 91
complex receptors, 17
conchae, 46
conduction deafness, 105
cones, 72, 73, 85–86, 87, 89
conjunctiva, 60–61
conjunctivitis, 61
contact chemoreceptors, 42
cornea, 67–68, 72, 81
corneal transplants, 72
crista ampullaris, 113
cristae receptors, activation of, 113–114
cupula, 113
cyclic adenosine monophosphate (cAMP), 52

D

dark adaptation, 91–92
deafness, 105
decibel (dB), 96
dehydration, 118–119, 122–124
dendrite, 17
dermal papillae, 26
diabetes insipidus, 124
diabetes mellitus, 74, 76, 124
digestive system, baroreceptors in, 25
dim light vision, 69, 72, 91–92
diplopia, 63
distance chemoreceptors, 45
distant vision, 81
diuresis, 120
dogs, olfaction in, 46, 47
double vision, 63

drives (motivational states), 116
drugs, and pain perception, 18
dynamic equilibrium, 109–110
dysgeusia, 42

E

ear. *See also* equilibrium; hearing
    inner, 100–103, 104. *See also* vestibular apparatus
    middle, 98–99, 100
    outer, 97, 103–104
ear canal, 97
ear drum (tympanic membrane), 97
edema, 125
electromagnetic energy, 59
electromagnetic spectrum, 79
emmetropia, 84
emotional reactions to smell, 54
encapsulated nerve endings, 26–29
endolymph, 100
energy balance, 125–126
epicanthal fold, 60
equilibrium, 109–115. *See also* vestibular apparatus
    dynamic, 109–110
    overview, 114–115
    receptor activation, 111–112, 113–114
    static, 110, 111
    structures for sensing of, 109–111, 112–113
exteroceptors, 17
extrinsic eye muscles, 64
eye, accessory structures, 57–66
    conjunctiva, 60–61
    extrinsic muscles, 64
    eyebrows, 57–58
    eyelids, 58–60
    lacrimal apparatus, 61–64
    overview, 64–66

eye color, 70
eye function, 79. *See also* sight; vision
eye movements, 64
eye structure, 67–78
    anterior cavity, 74–75
    lens, 75–76, 80, 84
    overview, 76–78
    photoreceptors, 72–73, 85–86
    posterior cavity, 74
    sensory tunic, 69–72
    tunica fibrosa, 67–68
    tunica vasculosa, 68–69
eyebrows, 57–58
eyelashes, 60
eyelids, 58–60

F

farsightedness. *See* hyperopia
fast pain, 30
feeding center, 127
fight-or-flight response, 54
filiform papillae, 36
floaters, 85
fluid balance. *See* water balance
focal distance, 80
focal length, 80
focal point, 80
focusing of light, 80–81, 84
foliate papillae, 35
fovea centralis, 72–73
frequency (sound), 95
fungiform papillae, 35

G

ganglion cells (retina), 70
general anesthesia, 18
general senses, 22–33
    and autonomic regulation, 25
    defined, 17

encapsulated nerve endings, 26–29
    overview, 32–33
    pain reception, 16, 18, 30–32
    pressure reception, 24–25
    proprioception, 17, 28–29
    stretch reception, 25
    temperature monitoring, 22–23
    touch reception, 23–24, 26–27
    unencapsulated nerve endings and, 22–25, 27
    vibration reception, 26
glands of Zeis, 60
glaucoma, 75
glomeruli, 53
glucostat hypothesis of hunger, 127
Golgi tendon organs, 29
granule cells, 53
green cones, 89
gustation, 34
gustatory cell, 36

H

hair cells (organ of Corti), 101, 104–105
hair cells (vestibular apparatus), 111
Hansen's disease, 28
hearing, 94–108. *See also* ear
    loss of, 105
    overview, 107–108
    physiology of, 104–106
    sensory coding in, 106–107
    sound transmission in, 103–104
heart attack pain, 32
heat perception, 22–23
hertz (Hz), 95
hunger, 116, 125–128, 130
hunger contractions, 126

hyperopia, 82
hyperphagia, 127
hypogeusia, 41
hypothalamus, 53, 54, 119, 127
hypotonic hydration, 125
hypovolemia, 126. *See also*
    dehydration
hypovolemic shock, 124

I
incus, 99
inner ear, 100–103, 104, 112.
    See also vestibular apparatus
insensible water loss, 117
interoceptors, 17
intrafusal fibers, 28
ions, cell membrane permeabil-
    ity to, 13, 52
iris, 69, 70
ischemia, 31
itch sensation, 27

J
juxtaglomerular apparatus, 119

K
kidneys, 121–122
kinocilium, 111
knee jerk reflex, 29
Krause end bulbs, 26

L
labeled line code, 18
labyrinthitis, 112
lacrimal apparatus, 61–64
lacrimal canals, 63
lacrimal caruncle, 60
lacrimal gland, 62
lacrimal puncta, 64
lacrimal sac, 64
lacrimal secretion, 62
lateral commissure, 59
lateral inhibition, 27

lens, 75–76, 80, 84
leprosy, 28
leptin, 127–128
light
    focusing of, 80–81, 84
    properties of, 59, 79–80
    refraction of, 80, 81
light adaptation, 90
limbic system, 53–54
lingual papillae, 35
lobule (ear), 97
loudness of sound, 95–97, 107
lysozyme, 62

M
macula lutea, 72
macula sacculi, 111
macula utriculi, 111
maculae, 111
maculae receptors, activation
    of, 111–112
malleus, 99
mate selection, pheromones
    and, 50
mechanoreceptors, 16, 41
medial commissure, 59
Meibomian glands, 60
Meissner's corpuscles, 26
melanin, 70
membranous labyrinth, 100
menstrual cycles, 50
Merkel disk, 23
metabolic water, 117
metallic taste, 39
microvillae, 36
middle ear, 98–99, 100, 112
mitral cells, 53
modality, 14, 15–16
monosodium glutamate (MSG),
    39
motion sickness, 113
muscle spindles, 28–29
Mycobacterium leprae, 28

myelin sheath, 30
myopia, 82

N

nasal cavity, 46–47, 64
nasal septum, 46
nasolacrimal ducts, 63, 64
near vision, 84
nearsightedness. *See* myopia
nerve endings, encapsulated vs. unencapsulated, 22–29
neurons, conduction in, 12–13, 52
neuropeptide Y, 127, 128
nictitating membrane, 61
night blindness, 88
night vision, 69, 72, 91–92
nociceptors, 16, 30

O

obesity, 127
obligatory water loss, 117
odorants, qualities of, 51–52
olfaction. *See* smell, sense of
olfactory bulbs, 52, 53
olfactory cells, 47–49
olfactory cilia, 49
olfactory epithelium, 47–49
olfactory glands, 49
olfactory nerve, 49
olfactory pathways, 53–55
olfactory region, 47–49
olfactory tracts, 53
opsin, 87, 88
optic disk, 70
optic nerve, 70
orbit, 57
organ of Corti, 101, 104–105
osmoreceptors, 15–16, 119
ossicles of ear, 99, 103
otitis media, 100
otolithic membrane, 111
otoliths, 111

otosclerosis, 105
outer ear, 97, 103–104
oval window, 99

P

Pacinian corpuscles, 26
pain
    classification of, 30–32
    perception of, 16, 18, 30–32
    phantom, 19
    receptors for, 16, 30
    role of, 16, 28
    tolerance of, 29
palpebral fissure, 59
papillae of tongue, 35–36
perception, 10–11
perilymph, 100
phantom pain, 19
phasic receptors, 19
pheromones, 50
photochemical reaction, 59
photons, 80
photoreception, 57, 87–89
photoreceptors, 16, 72–73, 85–86. *See also* cones; rods
pinna (auricle), 97
pitch of sound, 95, 106–107
posterior cavity (eye), 74
posterior chamber, 74
presbyopia, 76, 84
pressure receptors, 24–25
proprioceptors, 17, 28–29
prostaglandins, 18
pupil, 69
pupillary reflex, 69

R

receptor potentials, 13
receptors, sensory. *See* sensory receptors
red cones, 89
referred pain, 32
refraction, 80, 81

refractive index, 80
renin, 119
respiratory tract cilia, 51
retina, 69–72
retinal, 87–88
retinal detachment, 73
retinopathy, 76
rhodopsin, 87
rods, 72, 85–86, 87–89
root hair plexuses, 23
round window, 101
Ruffini's corpuscles, 28

S

saccades, 64
saccharin, 38
saccule, 109, 110–111
salty taste, 38
satiety center, 127
scala media, 101
scala tympani, 101
scala vestibuli, 101
scanning movements, 64
Schwann cells, 26, 30
sclera, 67
scratching, 27
seasickness, 113
semicircular canals, 112
semicircular ducts, 109, 112–
    113
sensation, 10–11
sense organs, 17
sensorineural deafness, 105
sensory deprivation tank, 15
sensory modality, 14, 15–16
sensory neurons, 17
sensory projection, 19
sensory reception, 11, 19
sensory receptors
    adaptation by, 19–20, 53,
        90–92
    classification of, 15–17
    overview, 20–21

role of, 11–12
    specificity of, 13–15
    transduction by, 13
    transmission by, 17–19
sensory receptor types
    baroreceptor, 25
    chemoreceptor, 15, 25, 34,
        41, 42, 45
    complex vs. simple, 17
    exteroceptor, 17
    interoceptor, 17
    mechanoreceptor, 16
    nociceptor, 16, 30
    osmoreceptor, 15–16, 119
    phasic, 19
    photoreceptor, 16, 72–73,
        85–86. *See also* cones;
        rods
    proprioceptor, 17, 28–29
    thermoreceptor, 16, 22–23, 41
    tonic, 20, 23
sensory tunic, 69–72
serous glands, 36
sight, 79–93. *See also* eye struc-
    ture; vision
    abnormalities in, 63, 82, 88,
        91
    age-related changes, 74, 76,
        84
    light and dark adaptation,
        90–92
    light focusing and, 80–81, 84
    light properties and, 59,
        79–80
    overview, 92–93
    photoreception, 57, 87–89
    photoreceptor anatomy,
        85–86
    refraction and image forma-
        tion, 81
    visual pigments in, 87
signal transduction, 13
simple receptors, 17

skin, sensory receptors in,
22–23, 26–27
slow pain, 30
smell, sense of, 45–56
    age-related changes in, 52
    in dogs, 46, 47
    loss of, 51
    neural pathways for, 53–55
    odor sensations, 49–52
    olfactory region structure,
      47–49
    overview, 55–56
    pheromones and, 50
    receptor location, 46–47
    role of, 45–46
    sensitivity of, 45
    taste and, 41
    transduction during, 52–53
somatic pain, 30
sound
    localization of, 107
    loudness of, 95–97, 107
    pitch of, 95, 106–107
    properties of, 94–95
    transmission to inner ear,
      103–104
sound wave, 95
sour taste, 38
special senses, 17. *See also*
    equilibrium; hearing; sight;
    smell, sense of; taste
spectrum, 79
stapedius, 99
stapes, 99
static equilibrium, 110, 111
stereocilia, 101, 104–105, 111
stimulus, 10, 19
strabismus, 63
stretch receptors, 25
sty, 60
supporting cells, 37, 47
suspensory ligament of lens, 75
sweet taste, 37–38

T

tactile sensation. *See* touch
    receptors
tapetum lucidum, 69
tarsal plate, 60
taste, 34–44
    age-related changes, 34, 40
    inherited sensitivity of, 40
    loss or distortion of, 41–42
    overview, 43–44
    receptor cells, 36
    receptor location, 34–36
    sensation types, 37–39
    smell and texture in, 41
    taste buds and, 34, 36–37
    tongue sensory map, 39–42
    transduction during, 42
taste buds, 34, 36–37
taste hairs, 36
taste pore, 36
tears, 62, 63
tectorial membrane, 103
temperature monitoring, 22–23
tensor tympani, 99
thalamus, 53
thermoreceptors, 16, 22–23, 41
thirst, 116–125. *See also* water
    balance
    in disease conditions,
      122–125
    drives and, 116
    in estimation of water bal-
      ance, 121
    overview, 129–300
    satiation of, 120–121
    water balance and, 116–117
    water intake/output regula-
      tion, 118–122
thirst center, 119, 120
tickle sensation, 26, 27
tinnitus, 100
tongue, 35–37, 39–42
tonic receptors, 20, 23

touch receptors, 23–24, 26–27
transduction, defined, 13
transmission, 17–19
trans-retinal, 87–88
tunica fibrosa, 67–68
tunica vasculosa, 68–69
tympanic cavity, 98
tympanic membrane, 97

U
umami taste, 38–39
unencapsulated nerve endings,
    22–25, 27
urine volume, 122, 124
utricle, 109, 110–111
uvea, 68–69

V
vesicles, 42
vestibular apparatus. *See also*
    saccule; semicircular ducts;
    utricle
    components of, 109–110
    cristae receptor activation,
        113–114
    maculae receptor activation,
        111–112
vestibular membrane, 101
vibration receptors, 26
visceral pain, 31
visible spectrum of light, 59, 79
vision. *See also* eye structure;
    sight
    abnormal, 63, 82, 88, 91

age-related changes, 74, 76,
    84
    close, 84
    of colors, 87, 89, 91
    in dim light, 69, 72, 91–92
    distant, 81
    light and dark adaptation,
        90–92
    role of, in humans, 57
vision loss
    cataracts and, 74
    corneal injuries and, 72
    glaucoma and, 75
    night blindness, 88
    retinal detachment and, 73
    retinopathy and, 76
visual acuity, 85
visual pigments, 87
vitamin A, 88
vitreous humor, 74
volume depletion, 122
vomeronasal organ, 47

W
water balance, 116–125
    during cold weather, 126
    disorders of, 122–125
    intake regulation, 118–121
    output regulation, 121–122
    overview, 116–117, 129–130
    thirst in estimation of, 121
water intoxication, 125
water taste receptors, 39
wavelength, 95

About the Author

Douglas B. Light is an accomplished educator who holds degrees in biology (B.A.), zoology (M.S.), and physiology (Ph.D.). His academic career began at Winslow High School in Maine, where he taught biology. He joined the faculty at Ripon College in Ripon, Wisconsin, in 1989 and taught general biology, anatomy and physiology, and immunology. He is presently professor of biology at Lake Forest College in Lake Forest, Illinois, where he teaches courses in organismal biology and animal physiology. He also conducts research designed to elucidate the mechanisms regulating transport of substances across biological membranes and how cells maintain their proper size. He has received more than half a dozen awards for his teaching and research excellence, and has been the recipient of several major grants from the National Science Foundation. He also has published more than a dozen articles in scientific journals, and has presented his research findings at numerous scientific conferences. Light is a member of several scientific and professional organizations, including the American Physiological Society, the Society for Integrative and Comparative Biology, and the Society of General Physiologists.